This book is dedicated to

Mrs. Lillian Mc Elroy

(A very wonderful and understanding friend.)
(I would have liked to have known her deceased husband)

To Eula, my wife

(A very sincere person who has become the achiever,
something that she thought was never possible)

Love, James

I wrote this book to inspire and encourage those that think that such adverse circumstances involving violence, hunger, poverty, drugs and financial uncertainty is their hopeless place in life. Troubles and trials come to us all but they must not control our life. If we live each day with a kind heart, with a "never quit" attitude we will overcome.

It is my sincere desire that a positive attitude with determination and hard work will impact one's inner strength to conquer adverse circumstances and become a Man.

I want this book to be an inspiration of hope to those who think that they are hopeless.

This is for those who want to be a man.

I would also like to thank the county of Allegheny and the state of Pennsylvania for feeding me, clothing me and seeing to it that I was in the best of health while I was in their care. Sometimes such places are needed to serve the best interest of children who are in need of a helping hand. With that help I grew up to become a productive member of society.

Contents

Chapter 1:	Abject Poverty In My Young Life (Hopelessness)	1
Chapter 2:	I Don't Understand, I Didn't Do Anything	5
Chapter 3:	Food, Food, My Kingdom For Some Food	6
Chapter 4:	My Savior (so I thought)	8
Chapter 5:	Thorn Hill: Youth Development Center at Warrendale	..12
Chapter 6:	Back On The Block	14
Chapter 7:	Morganza: Youth Development Center at Canonsburg	..16
Chapter 8:	Job Corp: Morganfield Kentucky	20
Chapter 9:	My Mother Hasn't Changed, So I Have To	23
Chapter 10:	Returning The Favor To My Sister	26
Chapter 11:	The Army And Freedom	30
Chapter 12:	Home On Leave	37
Chapter 13:	Vietnam 1969 – 1970, Smitty	39
Chapter 14:	The Shocking Revelation Of The U.S. Army Comradeship	47
Chapter 15:	The Court-Martial	49
Chapter 16:	Back In The World	51
Chapter 17:	Tae Kwon Do	56
Chapter 18:	My Fearless Attitude: I Will Not Quit	58
Chapter 19:	Los Angeles: Reading, Learning, Studying, Opens Successful Doors	60
Chapter 20:	NASA: Successful In All My Endeavors	62

CHAPTER 1

Abject Poverty in My Young Life (Hopelessness)

I DON'T KNOW WHAT I DID WRONG. I DON'T UNDERSTAND WHY MY MOTHER is doing this to me. I wish someone would help me. I was being thrown around, kicked, slapped, yelled at and I didn't know why. Finally, my mother started stepping on my neck while saying that she is going to kill me for causing so much trouble. What was the trouble that I was causing? A man who was supposed to be my father was coming to see me and I needed to be cleaned up because too many times he had come by to see me and I was dirty. This man (Buster) always let my mother know that he didn't appreciate my being dirty by beating her up. I was about four or five and the fighting was a constant everyday reminder to my mother that if I wasn't clean then she would be beaten up. My mother was pretty and always fought other women and men but it was Buster that made her shake with fear. When she knew that Buster was coming, my mother would hurriedly clean up the house and get my sisters and me all cleaned up. I was my father's favorite and I always remember him picking me up and inspecting me for any bruises and he would say "are you ok Jimmy" or "did you have enough to eat". I guess that I was a reminder to my mother that she had forgotten to clean me up and that Buster was coming so rather than clean me up she would kill me and that way she wouldn't have to deal with Buster anymore. I felt the pressure on my neck from her foot as she continue to push down at the same time saying die, die. I started to black out when I heard my mother scream in pain. My sister (Diane, who is older than I am) had grabbed my mother around her ankle and was biting her, trying to get her to stop stepping on my neck. For that act, my sister was punched, kicked and stomped. I couldn't do anything to help her because I was little and I was weak from being stepped on, so I just watched. To this day I am very thankful that my sister saved my life because later on I would return the favor. After my mother grew tired of beating my sister she saw that I had not moved and thought that she had killed me. She picked me up and said that she was sorry and started to clean me up.

There was a knock at the door. It was Buster. He came in and immediately sensed that something was wrong. I heard him ask my mother where I was and she told him. I started crying when he picked me up and he could see the foot print on my neck and he got very angry. Buster also saw how beat up my sister was. He told us to go outside for a little while. While outside we heard all of the commotion, the cursing and the obvious sounds of someone being beaten. After Buster left, my mother called us all back in and stated that we are going to move. The purpose of the move I believe was to escape from Buster. I never saw him anymore after we moved.

We lived in the Hill District section of Pittsburgh, Pennsylvania. This part of the city was where most black families lived who was poor. There were other sections of the city that had this type of ghetto for poor black families. There was Manchester (on the North Side) Northview Heights, Homewood, St. Clair Village or Whiteside Road. If you were black, nine times out of ten you lived in one of these areas. The Hill District was typical of a ghetto area. There were bars and pimps all up and down Center Avenue. There were Cadillac Eldorados and Fleetwood Broughams lined up and down the main drag, which was Center Avenue. Every week was like a parade to see who had the best Cadillac or who dressed the best. There were fish places and confectionary stores and places where you could buy three chicken wings for a quarter. People stayed out until the wee hours of the morning drinking gambling and just having a good time. It was well known that on Friday and Saturday nights the pimps and prostitutes ran the Hill District. By Sunday morning all of the hustlers were gone and the good people of the Hill District came out to go to church and pray for the sinners. This was where I grew up; this was my home.

There were ten of us in my family. None of us had the same father. I was the oldest boy with two sisters older than me. It seem that we never had enough to eat. My mother loved to stay out in the streets days at a time while we stayed home waiting for her to return and hoping that she would bring some food with her when she got back. What food we had went to the smaller ones first and if there was anything left then we ate. I spent a lot of time drinking sugar water and eating plain bread. My mother was on welfare and so every two weeks she would get a check. As I understand it now, the more children you have, the more money that you would get. Not only that, but there was the surplus cheese, powered milk, cornmeal, flour, sugar, butter, lard and meat that was given to everyone on welfare every two weeks. When this food arrived we thought that we had died and gone to heaven because that meant that we could eat as much as we wanted. We didn't mind eating cornmeal mush because we knew that as long as we had sugar and powered milk that the mush would be sweet. We even started to learn how to cook. First my sisters tried to make biscuits but used too much baking power. The biscuits came out big and they looked good but they tasted sour because of the baking powder. We didn't care we just put syrup and butter on them and ate them anyway. Next when we did get a loaf of bread we would make the ghetto version of a grilled cheese sandwich, which was just put the cheese on the bread melt it and eat it. We would always save the plastic wrapper that the cheese came in because when the food ran out we would take the cheese wrapping from the refrigerator and each one of us got a small piece and we would chew on it. We found this out by accident one day when we were very hungry. What we also found out was that if you chewed it long enough you could even blow bubbles with it. That was done during very lean times when there was nothing but water to drink and you had to go to bed hungry. You could always tell when my mother received her check because we always had a large pot of beans to eat. We ate lima beans, butter beans, black eyed peas, great northern beans, and navy beans. Once again we would feast. When the beans turned sour, we would just add water to them and continue to eat because we knew that there was nothing else to eat. My mother loves to drink and set up the bar. That is one of the reasons that she would be gone for up to four days. When the money would run out, only then would she return home and most of the time she was drunk. We were happy to see her anyway.

After awhile, someone would call the police on us because my smaller brother and sisters would cry a lot because they were hungry. The police would come and sometimes bring us a little something to eat and as long as we didn't appear to be in any immediate danger they would leave us alone. But after continue complaints from the neighbors they would go looking for my mother and arrest her and take us to juvenile court. For us it was a blessing because we never dreamed that there was such a place as this that was clean and they even gave you food three times a day. I never heard of eating that often. I also never saw a shower before and I didn't know that you had to change into your night clothes to go to bed because we always slept in our clothes or underclothes. The one thing that we were all happy about was the food. There were many different kinds and plenty of it three times a day and all the milk that you can drink. I don't know how long we stayed at the juvenile facility but we were all sad to leave. We were returned to our mother. Things got back to normal again. No mother, no food and hungry. I notice that our older sister Virginia did not return home with us and I never knew why or what happened to her until years later.

Food & The Battle for Control of the Night

We moved to another part of the Hill District over on Wylie Avenue across from a bar called the "Old Folks Home". I thought that things would be better because at least now we seem to have more food. It wasn't. My mother always seems to have boy friends and there was a different one every other night. Buster never came around anymore. I seem to figure out that whenever my mother had new boy friends we seem to always have food for awhile so we didn't seem to mind (what could we do any way). These guys were nice and they never bothered us. I was around seven or eight and we moved again over to another apartment on Harpers way. Things started happening again. My mother would go out drinking and leave us home again for days at a time. The lady upstairs would feed us (sometimes) and complain to my mother about us not having any food and making too much noise. My mother would argue with the lady saying that she didn't ask her to feed us and to stay out of her business. We were yelled at and slapped and told to be very quiet and not make any noise when she was not there. We had mayonnaise sandwiches until the mayonnaise was gone and then we just had plain white bread. The baby drank what powdered milk we had and sugar water. Diane, my sister, did the best she could. While we were living in this new place, we found out that there were rats running around at night. We were scared and the rats were brave. We would leave the lights on all night hoping that that would keep them away. It didn't. They would come out in the kitchen and play and look for food. Every morning we would first have to look into the toilet to make sure that no rats were in the toilet bowl because that is where we always found them, in the water. At night we would take as many pots as we had and put them in the bed with us so that we could throw them at the rats when they would come out. But these rats were not scared of us. There were times when they would find a way to crawl up in the bed and try to bite us. So the older kids would stay awake while the little ones slept and take turns sleeping while we watched for the rats. After a couple of days my mother would return and we would try and tell her about the rats but she was too drunk to care and would threaten us with a whipping if any of the little ones got bitten. My mother's new boy friend suggested that he set up a couple of rat traps. After killing a couple of them, the rats moved to another apartment and we could hear them scurrying across the ceiling and in the walls.

Chapter 2

I Don't Understand, I Didn't Do Anything

ONE NIGHT AFTER MY MOTHER HAD BEEN GONE ABOUT THREE DAYS, she returned as usual drunk but this time she was bleeding from some wound in her arm. There was blood all over the place and I kept bringing her another wet rag to try to stop the bleeding. I was scared because I had never seen so much blood and I guess I was just staring at her. She called me over to her and asked me what was I staring at and I couldn't put it into words or I couldn't explain it fast enough and I just didn't know what to say. She picked up a beer bottle took a drink from it and then hit me in the head with it. I screamed and cried and she kicked and slapped me at the same time. My sister was too scared to move and I lay on the floor crying and I didn't know what I had done to cause this. My mother got up and started to wipe the blood from my head and told me that she was sorry and told me to go to bed. The lady upstairs called the police because she had seen my mother come home and also she had notice that my mother was bleeding very badly. The cops arrived and came to the conclusion that my mother needed to go to the hospital. They had to carry her up about fifteen steps to get on the street. I heard one of the cops say that "this bitch is heavy". The lady's husband from upstairs came down to clean up the blood. By that time the blood had started to quagulate and he had to use a dustpan to pick it up because it was as thick as chocolate pudding. The scars in my head are now a part of my physical person. I was sick for a couple of days. My mother put peroxide in my head to keep the germs away but I never went to the hospital. After about a week she picked the scab off of the wound (which was very painful to me) and said that I would be all right and that I shouldn't have made her do it.

Chapter 3

Food, Food, My Kingdom For Some Food

THE LADY UPSTAIRS GOT TIRED OF FEEDING US AND I SUSPECT THAT she is the one that called the police to come and get us. This was another of many times that we would become a ward of the court. We didn't care because we knew once again that at least there would be food and clean clothes. Once again we would be returned to our mother. And once again the cycle started over again, no mother, no food and hungry. I started going to school with my sisters Diane and Eloise. At first everything seem fine and normal. My mother was staying at home and even though we didn't have much to eat at least our mother was at home. I liked school because at school they gave you milk and I was always hungry so the milk always made me feel better. At lunchtime I went home to eat biscuits and syrup. My clothes were adequate but I was always cold. I had a jacket that was torn but at least it kept me a little dry on rainy days. Winter was a different story. Winters in Pittsburgh are very, very cold. My shoes had holes in them and I had to put newspaper inside my shoes to keep the snow out and my feet dry. Sometimes I didn't go to school at all because of the cold and neither did my sisters. The only room in our house that was warm was the front room and we would all crowd around the stove with blankets to keep warm. When the gas bill wasn't paid then we drank warm water (we used a hot plate to heat the water) and kept our clothes on to keep warm. My mother would say that she was going out to buy some food but she would once again be gone for about three days and would return with only a loaf of bread (she was always well fed). We had eaten everything in the house and the only thing that was left was a can of pumpkin pie filling and a half a pound of lard. We got the can opened and ate the pie filling (which wasn't sweet) and we were happy to have that. I found another way to occupy my time. I would go up stairs when my sister wasn't looking and sneak into the bedroom to my favorite spot, which was a corner that had a hole in the wall. I would take my little fingers and dig the plaster out and eat it. It would fill me up then I would drink water, which would bloat my stomach. No one could figure out why the hole was getting bigger and my sisters thought that the rats were doing it. One day my sister caught me eating the plaster and yelled at me. All I could say was that I was hungry. When my mother came home my sister told her that she had caught me eating plaster. My mother got real mad and slapped me and told me not to do it again. The next day was our lucky day. We had food. My mother had brought home a very large goodwill size bag of bread, cakes, donuts and rolls. As I later found out, there was a Jewish bakery down on 5th avenue that was giving away one and two day old bread, rolls, cakes or anything that you could carry with you. So this was where our supply of food came from for a while. To us we had food, to our mother, it meant that she didn't have to use her welfare check to buy us food. (*One of the first things that I did after I left home was to go to a restaurant and order me a meal. The meal consisted of mashed potatoes and gravy, peas and two pork chops. The reason that I did this was to see what it felt like to eat a meal without sharing anything on my plate with someone else. Next I ordered a whole bottle of Pepsi and drank it all. It felt and tasted good. I didn't have to cut, divide or split anything. I enjoyed it all*) Again she left us this time it was for about five days. This would be the last time that my brothers and sisters would be together. When the food ran out we were hungry again and we had nothing but water to drink and the house had no heat. The police came again and did not hesitate to take us to juvenile court. The girls went to the female section and the boys went to the male section of juvenile court. My life was starting to change.

Chapter 4

My Savior (So I Thought)

IN JUVENILE COURT THERE WERE TWO CLASSES OF BOYS. THEY HAD THE senior boys (12 to adult) and they had the junior boys (7 to 12). I was in the junior boys section. To me life wasn't so bad because you had clean clothes and you went to school and you had three meals a day. My brother and I were sent to Camp Sleepy Hollow. This was a place that was run by the county of Allegheny for boys and it was located about thirty miles outside of the city of Pittsburgh. Only twenty boys at a time were at this camp. It was located out near South Park not far from Bethel Park Pennsylvania. At this camp you had plenty of fresh air and plenty of food to eat. You went to school everyday and basically you just played all day. There were a lot of wild animals like pheasant, deer and wild turkeys. I even joined the cub scouts at this camp. I belonged to the wolf pack. We camped out and went on a lot of nature hikes. I wanted those times to last forever. My brother and I were transported back to the city to be introduced to a lady. It seems that this lady was interested in two boys. This lady appeared to be very nice and my caseworker asked us if we would like to go and live with her. The lady painted a very pretty picture. My brother and I would have our own room. We would be going to a very nice school that was close to home. We would be allowed to go out and play anytime that we wanted. Also we would have very nice holidays, especially Christmas. So we agreed to go (as the case worker stated, on a trial basis). But it was permanent. This was my first introduction to a Foster Home.

When my brother and I arrived at our new home we thought that the house was a palace. The lady and her husband were very nice. She showed us our new bedroom and backyard where we could play. I think that my caseworker enjoyed her hospitality so much so that she did not bother to talk to us about anything more. She just left. The first few days were uneventful.

Then things started to change. We had to get up at six o'clock in the morning to sweep the sidewalk. We had to mop the front porch and back porch. We had to learn how to do the dishes and we were not allowed to watch the television. This foster parent told us that we were sent here to work not to have a good time. We were glad to go to school and we hated to come home. Everyday there was something for us to do before we did our homework or ate. As for the food, we were given just enough to fill us up and you were not allowed anymore. We did not get to drink milk, which was for the cereal. We were only allowed to drink water. For lunch we were given one sandwich and that was all. I guess that was better than nothing. Then the hitting started. If you dropped something you were hit. If you did not know something you were hit. If the floor wasn't clean you had to do it over again and you were hit. If your clothes were dirty you were hit. I couldn't tell time so I was shamed and informed that I wasn't any good and that I would never be any good. We were constantly reminded that our mother wasn't any good because if she were, then we would not be where we were. I was caught going into the refrigerator and was slapped and told that I was not allowed to. There were a lot of times when I was very happy to just go to bed and go to sleep. Mind you, this was a Christian lady who made sure that we went to church every Sunday and to prayer meetings every Wednesday and when ever there was some sort of program at the church, made sure that I had the largest part to memorize. This lady had grandchildren. When they would come over they stole her money and blamed it on my brother and I and we got the beatings. We were called thieves and told that we were not to be trusted. My brother and I got beaten with a lot of different things. For example a leather belt, a two by four, broom sticks and even struck once with a cast iron skillet. These things left enormous bruises on our bodies. When we went to school, sometimes, I was too embarrassed to take gym class because of the bruises. In those days if you went to school with bruises it meant that your father or mother did what they were suppose to do and it showed the teachers that if you gave them any trouble, you will be dealt with when you got home. I tolerated a lot of the beatings and yelling. I was getting bigger and stronger. My brother and I was getting beaten often and put in the basement with the lights out and the door locked. I was always getting teased because my voice was high and it had not changed yet to a deeper tone. One day my caseworker came by the house to check on my brother and I. I thought that this is my chance to tell on the lady. (*My first lesson that I learn when dealing with grownups is "unless you have a way out you don't open your mouth.*) When my caseworker asks me if everything was all right I said no. I stated that we are always getting beaten for nothing. My foster mother sounded shock and stated, "James how can you tell those lies about me". I said because they are true. The caseworker didn't believe me and said that maybe I misunderstood what she was doing in trying to help me and when she left I was beaten again with a stick and put in the basement. My arms were sore. My back was sore. My head was sore from getting beat with a belt buckle. I decided to run away. I was thirteen. The police picked me up and returned me to the foster home. After they left I got another beaten and told that I would be sent to a reform school if I did it again. I started thinking, could it really be that bad at a reform school. The next day was rainy and I was on punishment and it was my turn to do the dishes. While I was at the sink, I reached for the faucet and a blue light touched my hand. I jerked my hand back because I thought that it was lightening. My hand and my arm started to tingle. I opened the cabinet door over the sink, looking for some kind of burn hole since the other side of the kitchen wall was the outside of the house. But there was none. I didn't want to tell my foster parent because every time I would tell her something she would say that I am lying. So I kept what had happened to me to myself.

Every morning I had to sweep the sidewalk and I would try to do it before the kids started going to school because they would tease me about it. It got to the point that the kids would wait for me to come out so that they could tease me about sweeping the sidewalk. Finally I just stopped doing it or pretend that I had done it already. For a while it worked. But then I got caught not doing it and I got hit with the broomstick. This time, I steeled myself against the blow that I knew was coming and it didn't hurt as much. I was continually hit as I left for school and it just so happened that a girl that I knew at school heard what was happening and waited for me. She asked me what was wrong with that woman and I said that she was crazy and we both laughed. After school I did not want to go back home but I went anyway and as soon as I came through the door I had to scrub down the steps. I didn't want to do it and I said why do we always have to scrub the steps and floor everyday and sweep the sidewalk everyday. My answer was a pot to the head and because I said so. I left the kitchen and started cursing to myself but she heard me and ran after me with a stick. I ran upstairs and when I got to the top of the steps I turned and looked at her. She told me to come back down and I said no because I knew that she was going to hit me with the stick. She started up the stairs and I turned and picked up the telephone that was sitting on a table at the top of the stairs. I was going to hit her with it if she got any closer. After she looked up and saw what I was going to do she stopped and told me to just go to my room and stay there. Things were changing and I didn't want to get hit anymore for anything. I was fourteen and I was big for my age. The food and the health care that I received at the juvenile facility had done its job of giving my body what it needed. I was growing up strong and at fourteen I could take what this lady could dish out and not cry and finally one day when she was hitting me I took the stick from her broke it and threw it down. Her response to that was to go and get a bigger stick and continue to hit me. When I took that stick from her and threw it away she ran and told her husband that I had tried to hit her. Her husband was a nice guy. He never said too much about anything. He just got up at five o'clock in the morning and went to work in the steel mill. When he got home he would eat and read his paper and that was his day. He did come up to me and ask me what happened and after I told him that I didn't want to get hit for nothing any more he just turned and walked away. Later on I heard them arguing. She was telling him that he should whip me for defying her and he was telling her that it was not necessary. The lady truly didn't like me after that because I did not cry and I just stood there and took the beatings and didn't say anything. I think that I wore her out.

A Way Out Of An Abusive Environment

One day she hit me with a pot because I didn't clean it good enough. That pot gave me a headache and I was seeing stars for the rest of the day. Right then I made up my mind that I was going to kill her and spend the rest of my life in prison. I knew that she liked to drink coffee so I went to the basement to find something to poison her with. I found a small bottle of liquid. I didn't know what was in it but to me it looked old enough to do something to her. So I put the bottle in my pocket and waited for the next time that she asked me to make her a cup of coffee. I didn't have to wait long. She called me and wanted me to fix her a cup of coffee. I took the small bottle and emptied it into the coffee pot and poured her a cup of coffee. She drank the coffee and about thirty minutes later (I learned how to tell time) she got very sick. I just waited for her to die and then I would be free from all of these beatings that she was giving to my brother and me. As is turned out she didn't die. She just got sick and the next day she got better. After a couple more days I ran away again. This time the police took me to juvenile court. My caseworker asks me if I wanted to go back and I said no. Since I was older I was sent to the senior boys section of this facility. The boys in this section were big or bigger than I was. There was a lot of fighting going on and most of the boys there were there for stealing cars and robbing people. I was there because I didn't want to go back to my foster home. I was there for three months before I was sent to the farm. The old name for the farm was Thornhill. The new name for the farm is the Youth Development Center at Warrendale, PA, (YDC).

Chapter 5

Thorn Hill

Warrendale is located about forty miles east of Pittsburgh. You are out in the country with nothing around but farm land. In those days, they believed in fresh air and hard work will build good character and a healthy person. When I arrived at YDC I immediately started thinking about the stories that I had heard about the place. You were made to work in the fields all day. You were beaten if you disobeyed the guards and you only got two meals a day. Also if you really gave them a problem you were sent to Morganza and if you were old enough you were sent to Camp Hill one step below going to the big house. As we were driving up the road I could see the columns of boys marching back from school or the fields. It seems to me that everybody was regimented. You could hear the cadence being counted and everyone was in step. You did not hear any laughing or see any horse play. There were about five or six cottages. Each cottage held about twenty boys. Some of the cottages had dormitories and the other cottages had individual rooms. I was assigned to cottage number thirteen (13). The people that ran the cottages were called cottage parents. They were men. Their job was to make sure that you did what you were told. To get you up and out of the cottage on time whether you worked in the field or went to school. The food was cooked somewhere else and brought to each cottage three times a day. You were allowed milk and graham crackers before you went to bed and you had to shower every night. That didn't seem so bad besides I like being clean. I was told to go and sit in the day room until the rest of the boys came in. About an hour later you could hear the boys coming in from school and the fields. Everyone wanted to see the new boy and find out where he is from. About one third of the boys were from Philadelphia and one third was from Pittsburgh and the rest were from different parts of Pennsylvania. The white boys were from places like Chambersburg or Mechanicsburg. We called them farm boys. When they found out that I was from Pittsburgh all of the boys from around my way came up and gave me five and said that they were glad to meet me. The boys from Philadelphia didn't have too much to say but the fact that I was a brother made it all right. Of course I knew that I was going to have to fight sooner or later. There was this thing about who is tougher and who is the baddest, Philly or Pittsburgh. Even the (white) farm boys got in on it. The way it starts is someone takes your food or says something about your mother or steals your clothes just to see if you are going to do anything about. If you don't do anything about it then everyone knows that you are a punk and that they can just walk over you. It was definitely looked down on you as a brother if you let a white boy do anything to you without making them pay. Now there were some very tough white boys there, and they gave you respect and no one black or white would mess with them because of that. This was my introduction into the hierarchy of reform school life. As I settled into this new environment I learned a few things about this institution. The county of Allegheny did not run the institution any more. The state of Pennsylvania took over and that is why the name was changed to Youth Development Center. The state felt that the county was treating the boys like full-grown criminals with the beatings and the fieldwork and deprivation of food and water at times and the solitary confinement. So since the state took over, everything changed and it was more like a summer camp. Of course you were going to have runaways and fights and I could deal with that. The food was better than I had eaten at home. I never told my friends that I liked the place and that it was better than I had at home. To everyone else this was a bad place and nobody in their right mind would want to stay here and eat state food……except me. Their loyalty was to their family mine was to the state for taking care of me. I stayed at YDC for eleven months and then I was returned to my mother, a bigger healthier young man.

CHAPTER 6

Back on the Block

MY MOTHER HAD MOVED AGAIN. WE WERE STILL LIVING ON THE HILL, this time on Bedford Avenue. I was fourteen and I was able to take care of myself. My mother wanted me to stay home and baby sit my two younger brothers (Melvin and Ronnie). I did it for a little while but I got tired of doing it. Things were the same even after all these years. No food, my brothers were hungry and my mother wanted to always go out. My sisters were not at home at this time. They were (like me) put in foster homes and I didn't know where they were. My mother was still drinking and coming home drunk. While my mother was home and since I didn't have any money, I would steal food so that my brothers could eat. Whatever I would steal I would take it home for my brothers but my mother would give them a bite and eat the rest up. She would then tell me to go out and get some more. I found out that my mother's brother had a restaurant down on Center Avenue. I went in to the restaurant and ask him if he could give me something to take back to feed my brothers. What I got from him was an hour long lecture on why he can't do it. If he did it once then my mother would want him to do it again and again. I listen and politely said thank you and left. I would never ask him for another thing even if I were dying. I stole a loaf of bread and some cheese and took it home to my brothers so that they would have something to eat. My mother and I didn't get along because she wanted me to baby sit and I was telling her that she should baby sit her own kids. She threatened to stab me and I picked up a brick and threw it at her and left the house. I was in the streets as much as I wanted to be. This is the life. I didn't have any nice clothes but I could do what I wanted. I would go down on Center Avenue and watch all of the pimps with their nice Cadillac Eldorados, and Fleetwood Brougham dressed in their silk suits with all of the pretty women. I started thinking about where did they get all of that money to have all of the pretty things that they have. So I started stealing cars and driving around to impress my friends and the girls we hung out with. My friend Carlos Delarosa and I would go out on the weekend to steal cars. Carlos told me that I was taking too long so he showed me how to pop the ignition and it only took six to eight seconds and all you needed was a screwdriver. With that knowledge I had a car anytime I wanted one. Later it became a crime to walk around with a screwdriver in your pocket. Eventually I got caught and was sent back to juvenile court and this time I was sent to Morganza, Youth Development Center at Canonsburg. This was the only co-ed in the state.

Chapter 7

Morganza

THIS PLACE WAS A LOT DIFFERENT FROM YDC WARRENDALE. THERE were girls there and the guys there were bigger and tougher. Plus the guys here were in for robbing stores and holding up people. I guess that made me a criminal, why else would they send me here. I was sent to cottage number five (5) which was the intake cottage for new boys. You stayed there until you were sent to one of the other line cottages. Later cottage five (5) was turned into a regular line cottage. Once again the cottages housed about twenty boys. You had the boys from Philadelphia and Pittsburgh and the boys from the middle of the state out in the sticks (farm boys). Everybody went to school except those who wanted to work in the fields. I went to school for a little while and then decided to work in the field. They put me on Dalbo's Detail. Mr. Dalbo use to be an inmate here when the county had the place back in the forties. He took us to some underground cells where they use to chain the boys when they were misbehaving. Mr. Dalbo told us that every week they had black Friday. That meant that some of the boys were going to Camp Hill and some of the girls were going to Muncy. He also said that you use to have to line up for inspection before you ate and no one went to school. Everyone had to work in the fields. He was given five years for stealing a cow and after he did his time they kept him on as a worker. He told us that Morganza was all self contained. They canned their own food had their own cows and had their own pigs and chickens and beef. Once the state took over everything changed and the girls and boys were treated more humanely and no more black Fridays. It was pretty rough. I really liked working on Dalbo's Detail. We were outside most of the time doing things around the farm. When it was time to bale the hay, our job was to throw the bales up on a wagon after the machine had baled it. During the winter, we had to put up snow fences to keep the snow drifts from blocking the road. There were times when I went to school. The classes were all right for a reform school. There was this teacher named Bill Fitzgerald who seemed to take an interest in me. He was pretty nice for a white guy. He liked jazz and introduced me to the Jazz Crusaders and Modern Jazz Quartet (MJQ). A lot of the brothers liked Mr. Fitzgerald because he wore the same type of clothes that the brothers wore on the street. He didn't like to wear the little button down short sleeve cotton shirts or the high water pants with white socks and penny loafers. He wore the expensive gaucho knit sweaters with silk pants and banlon knee high silk socks with Bally or Florsheim shoes. He smoked Kool cigarettes and didn't mind giving you a pack if you behaved properly. He seems to have some distain for authority and would rather be in some club listening to jazz. He was cool (for a white guy) and none of the brothers bothered him. One day as school was being dismissed for the day he ask me to stay after class for a few minutes. He ask me what was I going to do when I got out of this place and I said I don't know. He ask me if I had ever heard of the Job Corp. He stated that it is a new program that the government had started up where you can go and get a skill while the government pays you for doing it. He stated that there are a lot of different camps around the country and that I should try to get into one of them. Mr. Fitzgerald stated that it was better than hanging around on the street doing nothing and that I should think about it. I told him that I would think about it and I returned to my cottage. The guys in my cottage had started to form a gang called the Boomerangs. The reason was because the other cottages were picking on guys in our cottage and we had to do something to let them know that if they picked on one of us that they would have to fight all of us, including the white boys. To identify ourselves from a distance we would raise our arm above our heads and bend it slightly to the left or right depending on which arm you were using. We all prepared to do a lot of fighting to establish ourselves and to start holding a lot of check. If you held a lot of check you held power. As a gang we would hold a lot of check and within the gang there were checkholders. A checkholder was a person who could fight real good and would get things done and keep the other guys in line. Any new guy coming into the cottage had to be checked out to see if he could fight or not. If he could then we had another fighter on our side. If he couldn't then that meant that we just had another person to protect. That Monday at school things started up. One of our guys was being pushed around by some guys from cottage seven and the fight started. In order to get respect as a check holder you really had to do something outrageous when fighting someone else. Chairs were picked up and smashed on someone's back. When your opponent was down you had to stomp them to make sure that they wouldn't get up and finally since this was a co-ed place you had to take their girlfriend by saying she belonged to you. The girl had no say. That was the ultimate insult to a loser. There was so much constant fighting going on in school every day that the institution had to cancel classes to find out what was going on. The girls liked it and after a while we were known as the Rangs. The girls started giving us a little cheer leader show every time they saw us coming. We had already anticipated that some of us would be jumped by other cottages and beaten up. To counter act this, we would always keep coming back until we get you. That's why we liked the name Boomerangs, because we always come back. Everybody in the cottage that belongs to the Boomerangs had a nickname. These are the names of some of the guys that were Rangs. There was Lip from Homewood, Crip from Homewood, Dice from Philly, Fatback from Philly, The Player from South Philly, Crazy Joe from the Hill, Go Go from the Hill, The Hawk from the Hill and I was County from the Hill. Even now, forty years later my friends still call me and I am still known as County. We had heard that a guy named Joe Canada from cottage three was talking about me and that I was just a punk and he was going to get me on Monday. I was always known as the guy who didn't say much so I guess Joe thought that I was easy and that he could take me. The wolf tickets were being sold at every opportunity and it even got to the point that the girl cottages had started taking sides. There were five girl cottages and we had three of the cottages on our side. Each girl cottage held about fifteen girls so that was a lot of girls. What the girls liked about us was that we weren't afraid to challenge authority. When there was an assembly we were always the last to arrive and we never opened the door, we always kicked the door in which made a loud noise and disrupted everything. After a while we weren't allowed to go to the assemblies or to the movies that they showed on Saturdays. When Monday arrived we left the cottage early so that we could get to school first and set up on the front steps. We could see all of the cottages marching in twos coming toward the school. Everybody was ready for the anticipated fight. Our guys was spread out on the steps of the school blocking the doorway so no one could get in from the front. Even the white boys wanted a piece of the action. The white boys weren't afraid to fight, its just that they were not use to being around black people and a lot of them had never been around brothers before because they were from the center of the state, farm boys where all they saw were white people. After they saw that our blood was just as red as theirs they became good friends especially since they were in the cottage with us and we didn't let anybody mess with them. As I have said before, its not that we were so bad its just that we meant business. We saw cottage three (3) coming down the road and they knew what was up. We were ready. I heard the teachers talking from the upstairs window saying where are the students and why aren't they in class yet. One of the teachers must have looked out of the window because I heard her say that something is going on and it looks like a big fight is about to take place. Two of the white boys stuck a piece of wood in the door so that it could not be opened and did the same at the back door. The teachers started screaming at us to not fight. I heard one of the boys in cottage three say to Joe Canada that there is Clark and he doesn't look scared. They pushed Joe and told him to go ahead and get me. I left the steps and Clyde came with me and I got right up in his face and said that I heard that he was looking for me. He said yeah that's right and that he was going to kick my ass right here in front of all of these girls so that they can see that I'm nothing but a punk and that he was going to take my girlfriend from me after he's through. Right after that he swung on me with a left and right but I was faster and I bobbed and weaved and went down and jacked him up over my head and slammed him down hard on the ground. When you don't think about it, your body can move without you even knowing how you did it. I could see the fear in his eyes as I scrambled to get on top of him and started to punch him in his face and in his mouth. The blood started to come and I felt someone trying to pull me off of Joe. It was one of his boys trying to help him. I heard Clyde say get off of him. Clyde jumped in and punched the guy and they started fighting. Two of the girls who had boyfriends in cottage three started hitting Clyde and some of the other girls who were for us jumped them and beat them up. There were fights breaking out all over the place. I was beating Joe Canada so bad that I didn't realize that he was just holding on and wasn't fighting anymore. I stomped him once more and left him alone and went to see if Clyde needed any help. He didn't. By this time security had come and were trying to break the fights up. The teachers had finally got the door open and were out trying to calm things down. I got put into solitary confinement along with Clyde and some of the other guys in my cottage because we were the instigators (so they say). After that fight we were checkholders on the whole farm. Everybody wanted to transfer to cottage five. The girls loved us and everybody wanted to say that they had a boyfriend in number five. When we went to school, everybody wanted to slap five with us and just nod their head to show that they recognized us. Even our cottage parents got more respect from the other cottage parents. At this facility we were allowed to have dances twice a month. Everybody wanted to come to our cottage to dance because we gave the best dances. (Not really, we just treated the girls better.) After getting out of solitary confinement I was taken off of Dalbo's Detail and kept in school. I told Mr. Fitzgerald that he was right and that I wanted to go to the Job Corps. He said ok he would get the paper work started. After about a month Mr. Fitzgerald informed me that I had been accepted into the Job Corps and that they would be sending me a letter letting me know where I would be going. Also by joining the Job Corps it helped me get out of Morganza very quickly. Within a month I was back home with my mother.

Chapter 8

Job Corps

I DIDN'T DO ANYTHING AT HOME. I JUST BABY SAT WHILE MY MOTHER ran the streets. I was fifteen. I drank instant coffee all the time so that I could stay up to let my drunken mother in. Finally the letter came and I found out that I was going to Breckenridge Job Corps Center in Morganfield, Kentucky. I was happy to just get away. They had sent me a ticket and three days later I was on my way to Kentucky. I didn't have to bring anything with me. They would supply everything that I would need.

    I arrived at the Job Corp Center in Morganfield Kentucky in the early afternoon. This was the place where they housed the 101st Airborne Division. There were barracks everywhere. I had chose electronics as the subject that I was interested in. This was the time when computers were just started to make their break though. This was the days when one computer took up a whole room. So I chose computers and as it turned out the only computer classes were in Massachusetts and they didn't have any openings at the time. So I decided to stay in electronics and do motor rewind. I was in area three the orange area. That was my color. Every area of training had a different color. For example, automobile repair's color was blue, masonry was brown etc. Everything in that area was painted that particular color so that you knew where you were. I was shown where my barracks were and given a green uniform, under clothes, shoes and socks. I was shown where the mess hall was located and told that it was my responsibility to get there eat and go to class on my own. No one was going to wake me up and make sure that I washed up and was wearing the proper uniform to class. No one was going to do my laundry for me or iron my clothes. I was there because I wanted to learn something so the responsibility was mine and mine alone and I could leave anytime that I wanted. You would be given a stipend of twenty-five dollars every two weeks for what ever you wanted to use it for. Also if you told them that you wanted to save seventy-five dollars they would match the seventy-five dollars and you would be saving one hundred and fifty dollars a month. Another option was that you could have that money sent to a bank or to your home. I thought that this is great. I could help my mother by letting her keep half, because I know that she could use the money and saving my other half which will be seventy five dollars. I figured that I could save up a lot of money that way. So I told them to send my money home. After a couple of weeks my mother wrote me a letter telling me that she had in fact received the one hundred and fifty dollar check. She told me that she had brought food and a few things that were needed around the house. Every month she told me that she had brought something different. I felt good that I was helping my mother and that my brothers were at least eating well. My classes were broken down into two week blocks. Every two weeks you were moved to something different provided that you understood everything that was taught within that two week period. The teachers were German. They told you their name and got right down to teaching. I had to first learn basic electricity. They put everything on the blackboard. I took many notes because I didn't know what they were talking about. I was in over my head but I wanted to lean and I didn't have anything else to do and since that was why I was there I made myself study. In the end all I could think of was "I did it". From that point on I knew that knowledge was a blessing.

Learning basic electricity was not hard. The hard part was learning the geometry and trigonometry. The teachers didn't ask if you knew any, they just put it down on the black board and they expected you to learn it. I learned about Ohm's law (the voltage times the resistance) $E = I/R$, $R = I/E$, I E/R. E stood for voltage. I stood for current and R stood for resistance. I learned about the little striped things in the back of transistors were called resistors. The different colors on the resistors meant something. I learned about the color code which stood for: Bad Boys Rape Our Young Girls But Violet Gives Willingly. The colors were: Black Brown, Red Orange Yellow Green Blue Violet Grey and White. The instructors would put an equation on the board and we would have to pick out the right resistor with the proper color code on it and put it on the trainers in front of us. If the little red light lit up you knew that you had the right color coded resistor. By the time I got to block three I was doing fine, I thought. There were two solid blocks of trigonometry. I had to take block three over again. I didn't mind. For recreation we had football and softball teams. There were even times that we went to St. Louis to a girls Job Corps Center. We were even allowed to go to Evansville Indiana to just go into town to do something different. I had been receiving letters from my mother telling me how wonderful things are going and to keep sending her the money. I had calculated that by this time that my share of the money being sent home was five hundred dollars.

I figured that I could do a whole lot with that money. In the mean time I had been talking with the army recruiter there at Breckenridge. I had told him that I wanted to be a paratrooper and could he get me in it. He ask me how old I was and I told him that I was fifteen and a half. He told me that if I waited a little bit longer until I was sixteen and if I could get my mothers signature to sign me in then I could join up. Since I was almost sixteen anyway he signed me up under the ninety day delay enlistment program. Which meant that I could sign up but that I didn't have to go in for three months. It was something new. I figured that this was perfect. I could leave the Job Corps and go into the army. I could go home visit my friends and see how well my mother is doing with my help. I had five hundred dollars saved up and with the money that I would be getting from the army I could keep on saving. I also knew that I would not have any problem getting my mother to sign me up. So I left the Job Corps.

Chapter 9

My Mother Hasn't Changed (A Great Disappointment): So I Have To

It took about a day and a half for me to reach Pittsburgh. I arrived in the afternoon about three o'clock. When I got home and knocked on the door my little brothers opened the door. When I ask them where our mother was, of course they didn't know. But that wasn't the half of it. I was totally shocked at what I saw. First of all there wasn't any new furniture as my mother had told me. There was no food in the refrigerator. The house was dirty. I went upstairs and found that all of my clothes were gone. The first thing that went through my mind was I that I hope that she didn't spend my money. I needed an explanation so I sat down and waited. My mother didn't know that I was home so when she returned home at about six-thirty and opened the door her mouth dropped to the floor. Her first words were "what are you doing here"? I said that I was tired of being there and decided to come home. She said that I have to go back to the Job Corps so that she can keep getting the money that she needed for the house. I ask her what had she been doing with the money because everything is as it was when I left. That I saw nothing new and there was no food in the refrigerator. She said that she had bills to pay and I said what bills. She told me that someone had broke into the house and stole all of the new furniture. I knew that she was lying. She told me that I could not stay there and that I would have to get out. I said fine just give me my five hundred dollars, which is half of the money that she was suppose to be saving for me. She told me flat out that the money was hers because her name was on the check. I told her that she would've never got the money if I hadn't told them to send it. I was very mad. I knew that she had spent the money. There wasn't any money. I was broke. I didn't have a thing. I just left and started to walk down to Center Avenue. As I turned the corner, in the window in front of me was my trench coat and some cuff links that were given to me as a going away present from my girlfriend from Morganza. My mother had pawned or sold all of my things. I saw my friend Gunzee. We had been together since we were little. He was happy to see me and said that he had something to tell me. I ask him to tell me. He said man, your mother has been setting up the bar all week and telling everyone that her son is taking care of her. That kind of hurt me real bad but I knew that it was true. I didn't feel like talking anymore so I left Gunzee and just walked around the Hill for a little while. I decided to walk to the Oakland section of Pittsburgh to my aunt's house to see if I could spend the night. My aunt was an ok person. She just stayed in her own little world and didn't bother anyone. I stayed there until the next morning and walked back to the Hill. I had to have something to do until my papers come from the army so I went back home. My mother was happy to see me but not because she was worried about me but because she wanted to go out and didn't have a baby sitter. She thought that she was doing me a favor by saying that I could stay there as long as I didn't eat any of her food. I agreed and told her that I am just staying until my military papers came. She ask me if I had any money and I said that I only had five dollars when in fact I had fifty dollars. She told me to give her the five and she will give it back to me later when she returned. I knew that I wouldn't see the money again and it was worth it to just give it to her just to get rid of her. The mailman came later that day and delivered the letter that I was waiting for. I still needed her signature because I was still under age. I was sixteen. My mother returned around two in the morning drunk as usual and I told her that I needed her signature to join the army. She said that she would sign the papers if I did one thing for her. What she wanted was for me to sign over my military insurance to her as my beneficiary in the event that I got killed. I quickly agreed, but I had no intention of ever doing that but the thought of me getting killed and her getting ten thousand dollars made her sign quickly. She told me that I should be a marine. I told her that I am going to be a paratrooper. Her only response was "yeah, they do a lot of fighting to".

 The next day I went down to the federal building with my paper work. Everything was ok. I took and passed the physical and got my free meal when they were through. They notice that I had joined under the delay enlistment program and if I wanted to continue to wait for another two months. I told them no, that I wanted to leave as soon as possible. They told me that I would be receiving a ticket in the mail in a couple of weeks and that they didn't know which fort that I would be going to. That was fine with me. I was getting off of the Hill and out of Pittsburgh. I was going somewhere. I was going to be a soldier. I just had to hang around my mother for another two weeks and not get in any trouble with her or the police. I didn't go out much. I just stayed in the house and watched my brothers while my mother went out with her new boyfriend Melvin. Melvin was ok. He didn't say much. He just stayed in bed and when the sun went down he and Mary would get dressed and go out drinking at different bars. They always would come home at about three or four in the morning after the bars would close. Of course there was arguing and fighting. I would always hear my mother say that if he touched her she would get me to beat him up. It seems that every time my mother brought some guy home I was supposed to be prepared to beat these guys up for something that she did. I would always leave because I got tired of hearing that coming from her. The next morning my mother would come in and ask if I could borrow some money from one of my friends so that she could buy cigarettes. I told her no. Then she said " why don't you go out and rob and steal like Chipper does and bring it all home to me." I said because I don't want to. I couldn't believe that my own mother was asking me to rob and steal. That made her mad. Chipper is the son of one of my mother's friends. He use to rob people and steal cars all of the time. I even caught him trying to talk to my sister Diane in the hallway once. I heard him tell her that the next time she saw him that he would be driving a pink Cadillac and dressed in a pink vine with (a vine is a suit) a pocket full of money. His rap and his game was lame. When he found out that Diane was my sister he kind of stayed away. I had to pull my sister's coat. I told her that he was nothing and that she shouldn't go with him because he was a bum. She didn't like what I had told her but she listened. A couple of weeks later, Chipper was involved in a robbery of a jewelry store and it was right next to where I lived. He and another guy name Bama Blues Man robbed the place and one of them shot the jeweler. I think Chipper got twenty years and Bama got life. I told my sister and she was glad that she left him alone.

Chapter 10

Returning the Favor to My Sister

When I was fifteen and living at home with my mother (one of the few times), my sister Diane came home from her foster home to live with us. I kept hearing my mother say how she was going to get us all back and that this was just a start. I thought that things would be better now that one of my older sisters was home. But it wasn't. At first everything seem normal on the surface. My sister and I would always walk to school together. We both went to 5th Avenue High School which was located on Dinwiddie and 5th Avenue. I could tell that my sister liked having me around her. We hadn't seen each other for at least ten years and I was happy to be with her too. We would do sister and brother things like share lockers and what money we had. I smoked Kools and she smoked Newports so if one of us ran out the other would always have a pack of cigarettes. After a while, things started to change. My mother would tell my sister to stay at home and watch our two little brothers while she went to the store. Which meant that she was going out drinking with Melvin. Everyday when I would come home my sister always had a worried look on her face. I didn't know what was going on so I didn't pay any attention to her. I think that this is where my mother started testing the water, to see what she could get away with. Anyway, as I came home each day I would notice bruises on my sister's arm or her face or her legs. I would ask her what happened and my mother would say that she got smart and that she had to put her in her place. I thought about it for a while and figured that since my sister was older than I was maybe something did happened. I would look at my sister and she would shake her head no, as that didn't happen the way my mother said it did. So I started paying a little more attention to detail and each day I would run home as quickly as I could. Every time I would come through the door my sister would run and hug me very tight so much so that I had to pry her hands off of me. I would notice that her dress would be torn and she would have bruises all over her. Once more I would ask her what happened and this is what she told me. Every day my mother would think of some reason to keep her home from school. My mother would leave and come home around noon drunk with some man. She would say that my sister was trying to entice this man and start beating her. She would knock her to the floor and kick her and punch her and start ripping her dress off of her. Diane said that these guy would just sit there and enjoy the show and do nothing. That was why she was always so happy to see me. After these incidents my sister started begging me not to go to school and to stay home with her. I had to know for sure if this was true, not that I doubted my sister, but I had to know. So I told my sister that tomorrow I would pretend to go to school and double back and wait until I see my mother leave and then I would trade places with her. She agreed. The next day I left early and waited until I saw my mother leave and then I went back to the house and switched places with my sister. It wasn't long before I heard my mother coming up the steps with some dude. When she got to the door I heard her say to the guy "just watch I'm going to beat this bitch and rip her clothes off". "You're going to see me stomp this bitch". I couldn't believe what I was hearing but it was true. When my mother opened the door and saw me her mouth dropped to the floor. She started stuttering and finally said what are you doing here? I said that I wasn't feeling well so I decided to come home so that Diane could go to school. That did it. I had blown her plans. She looked at the guy and he just turned and left. After that I never let my sister stay in the house by herself again. I always stayed home and watched our two younger brothers. My mother kind of figured out that I was staying home for a reason and she never tried to hit my sister while I was home. But that didn't stop her from going out and getting drunk and coming in around three o'clock in the morning. When she did she would make up some excuse to yell at my sister. My sister and I would have this little conversation every night at eleven o'clock. My sister would say "well I guess I'd better go to bed", and I would reply " yeah I guess you'd better before your crazy mother gets home". This night around three thirty my mother came home drunk and as usual I was up waiting for her and my sister was asleep in the bed in the back room. She came in and didn't say anything to me except that she had to go to the bathroom. I didn't think anything of it. After a few minutes I started wondering what was taking my mother so long to go to the bathroom so I decided to go and see. The way the apartment was made, you had to go through the kitchen and through the bedroom to get to the bathroom. When I got to the kitchen I could see my mother standing by my sister's bed with her arms raised above her head. As I got closer I could see that she had one of those large cast iron skillets above her head and she was going to bash my sisters head in. Everything happened at once. I yelled "what are you doing to my sister" and when I said that, my sister woke up and started to scream. My mother dropped the skillet and ran past me and ran out of the door. My sister was shaking violently and crying. All that she could say was that "she was going to kill me", "she was going to kill me" and "I never did anything to her". My sister kept saying "Jimmy why does she want to hurt me, I never did anything to her". All that I could say was I don't know, I don't know. Diane would not go to sleep. She would not sleep in that bed. If she wanted to make some coffee in the kitchen, she would not go in there unless I was with her. If she wanted to go to the bathroom I had to go and stand by the door because she would not close the door. If she wanted to take a bath I had to stand by the door. When she wanted to go to sleep, she would only sleep on my lap. After I thought that she was asleep I would carry her to her room and put her in the bed but she would wake up screaming for me. The irony of this was that I had just repaid my sister for saving my life when we were little. My sister was stuck to me. I was feeling awkward. This was my older sister. She should have the answers to this madness. My mind went back to when I would come home from school and find my sister beat up. I remembered my sister begging me not to go to school. I remembered my sister turning to see me when I would come home from school with more than just love in her eyes. I remember my sister running to me when I got home from school and squeezing me so tight that I had to pry her arms off of me. Finally I remembered how my heart felt when I believed what I saw with my own eyes and all that I could do was say that I was sorry and even that was not enough. I knew that I would always love and protect my sister from this woman. When my mother ran out of the door she was gone for three days. When she returned it was around midnight. My sister was asleep and I was sitting at the kitchen table drinking coffee. When my sister heard her coming she started to tremble and I had to calm her down by telling her that I would not let anything happen to her. My mother called us both into the front room and she didn't even acknowledge what she had tried to do three days ago. My sister was scared but she trusted me. My mother wanted us to join hands with her and make a small circle. Then she started mumbling something that didn't make sense and wanted us to repeat it. I refused to do it and told her that this was stupid. Of course she started to scream at me and call me names. I was sixteen. I was not afraid. I was big. I was strong and I was ready for her. I told Diane to go to her room and go to sleep that I would watch over her. My mother's reply to this was to reach behind one of the chairs in the front room and pull out a piece of lead pipe and hit me in the back with it. She was going to hit me again but I did not fall down. Instead I grabbed the pipe and twisted it until I got it away from her, pushed her down and started to hit her with it. Diane said "no Jimmy please don't do it". That is the only thing that stopped me. So what I did was take the pipe and bend it in half and threw it on the floor. I told my mother that she had better not ever touch my sister again. She did what I expected her to do. She told me to get out of her house and never come back and then she ran out of the door. My back was hurting where she hit me with the pipe. I took my shirt off and my sister saw a very large black and blue mark on my back. There was nothing that either of us could do about it. I told her to get what she wanted to carry because we are leaving. My mother, I found out was across the street at a bar called the Old Folks Home. She was drinking. My sister wanted to know what are we going to do with my little brothers. I told her that they are our mother's responsibility and lets go. So we left. I took Diane over to our aunts house in Oakland where we stayed the night. The next day after we had eaten we went our separate ways because she knew where she could stay and I didn't know where I could stay at the time and I didn't want to impose on the people that she would be staying with. I gave Diane my last three dollars and we said good-bye. I would not see my sister for about seven years. By that time she had met someone and had moved to Baltimore, Maryland.

CHAPTER 11

The Army and Freedom

FINALLY MY TICKET FROM THE MILITARY CAME. I WAS VERY HAPPY. I KEPT looking at the envelope. It said Private James W. Clark. I was really going to the army. I was going to take basic training at Fort Knox Kentucky. I thought to myself, didn't I just leave Kentucky. I told my mother that I would be leaving later on in the evening because that was when my bus left. All she could think of was don't forget to put me down as your beneficiary. I said ok and then I left. I really didn't have anyone to say good-bye to but to me that didn't matter because I was ready to leave. I left Pittsburgh around eleven p.m.. It took the bus about one day to reach Fort Knox. While enroute to Fort Knox Kentucky by bus, we stopped at a bus station which was a rest stop. I went to the cafetera and ordered a chef salad. When the salad was brought to my table, I noticed that there were pieces of what I believed to be hard stale bread on it. I was a young black kid who had never been anywhere and I didn't know anything about the different types of food. I immediately took offense because I thought that someone was trying to get rid of some old stale bread and decided to give it to the black kid because black people don't know anything and they won't make a fuss. I sat there and pondered whether or not I should eat this salad or take it back and tell them that I don't want it because it has stale bread on it. I decided that I would show them (white people) and eat the salad and the stale bread. I figured that it didn't harm me when I ate stale bread at home and this would be no different. Beside, I had some milk to wash it down with. So I ate it. It tasted funny, like it had salt or something on it but I crunched through it. I even smiled at the white lady that I thought had given this to me. I finished the salad with the stale bread and left the cafeteria, satisfied that this was one black person that showed them that I was not fazed by their ignorance. It wasn't until a couple of years later that I found out about crotons. We never at crotons in the ghetto and when you're poor, stale bread is just that, old bread that's hard. I realized that I was the ignorant one and was happy that I didn't make an issue out of it. This was just one of many incidents that showed me that there is more to the world that I know than just poverty and violence. That is why I always read books and learned to listen whenever someone was speaking because you don't have to be a scholar to be a teacher and you don't have to be a student to learn. When we arrived it was dark. The drill instructors started screaming for every one to get off of the bus and line up straight. We spent the next several hours in orientation. We received our fatigues boots the rest of our gear. We filled out lots of paper work. When I was ask who did I want to be my beneficiary I didn't know what to say. I ask the lady what should I do. She told me to keep it in the family because many girls go out with these guys and hope that these guys put their girlfriends name down and when they get killed the family does not get any money. So I decided to put my sister Virginia's name down as my beneficiary. Of course we got all of our hair cut off. I was sent to Company C, 13th Battalion 4th Training Brigade. The first thing that we had to do was make our bunks. Next we had to put all of our military clothing away in the proper order. Finally we had to start scrubbing our barracks down. I found out that in basic training all you do is get ready for inspection every day. We were using and training with the M-14 rifle. We learned to assemble and disassemble it. We had to spit shine our shoes. Our day started at four o'clock in the morning. Eating was a joke. We had to take all that we wanted and we had to eat all that we took. I say that it was a joke because you were never given enough time to eat everything. You just shove it in and move out. When we got paid we couldn't go anywhere to spend your money. A lot of the trainees (that's what we were called) would send their money home. I would just keep mine. Basic training was eight weeks long. I finally got a good look at Fort Knox. It was the home of the armor division. There were a lot of tanks and big howitzers. All of the training brigades were almost one hundred percent black and I couldn't figure out why. Then it hit me. Most of these guys were from Detroit, Michigan. They drafted a lot of guys from this area. Around that time there was a big riot or something there so they either emptied out Detroit or a lot of brothers just wanted to get away. Everybody that I talked to told me that they were drafted. Their dog tag number started with a US. Mine started with an RA. RA meant Regular Army, it meant that you joined and were not drafted. So I trained. I slept in the rain under a poncho. I got to eat C-rations (which to me were pretty good). The C-rations had beef stew, cheese, fruit cocktail, cookies, spam, cocoa, matches, toilet paper and a couple of cigarettes. It was all right, It was food. When we were almost through with basic training an Airborne sergeant came to our barracks and gave us a pep talk about Airborne Training. At the end of his pep talk, he ask how many people wanted to join up. Of course I raised my hand. This was what I wanted. Out of a company of two hundred and fifty guys, only twenty of us raised our hands. He took down our names and that was the last we saw of him. We went to the rifle range to practice shooting our weapons. If you failed to hit your target, you would not graduate. The three shooting medals you could get was Marksman, Sharpshooter, and Expert. Shooting expert meant that you hit all of your targets. I shot expert. Not bad for a guy from the city. We trained and did KP duty. At night we shined our boots and got ready for inspection the next day. Finally graduation day arrived and we all were happy. There were a lot of girl friends and mothers and fathers and friends that showed up for the ceremony. I was very proud of myself in my uniform and my expert badge pinned on my chest. The ceremony lasted a couple of hours and everyone congratulated everyone else. Everyone was happy. It was time to move on. I was sent to Fort Dix, New Jersey to AIT (Advanced Infantry Training.) The war in Vietnam was heating up. At Fort Dix we learned infantry fighting tactics in the field. We were given M-16s. We learned about night fighting and how to throw grenades. At the firing range we were given tracers with our bullets. Most of the time at Fort Dix we were in the field. We practice bayonet training and hand to hand combat. Some of the guys that were training us had been in Vietnam already. To most of us the war was still far, far away. There were not as many inspections. Most of the time was spent on infantry tactics. We learned how to read a map and how to use a compass. We at plenty of c-rations. I had stopped smoking because of all of the physical training (PT). At least at this post you were allowed to go to the beer halls and drink beer. I had a couple but I didn't drink that much because I knew that we would have to work it off the next day. I was adjusting to military life. I was getting paid to do a job. The food wasn't that bad and I could wear my uniform. I was growing up. Once again a sergeant from the Airborne training school came by and ask who wanted to go Airborne. I raised my hand again. This time there were less people who wanted to go. They were saying that I was crazy for jumping out of a plane. I wanted to go and that was that. This time after talking to the sergeant I was told that when I finished AIT that I would be going to jump school at Fort Benning Georgia. I was satisfied with that answer. After another three weeks in AIT I received my orders to go to Fort Benning Georgia.

Jump School

When I arrived at Fort Benning it was about three o'clock in the morning. The drill instructors were yelling at us like we had just joined the army. It was dark and although I couldn't see anyone, I heard commands being given and the troops were running. Thump, thump, thump thump, that was all that you heard in the dark boots running. Then I heard the Airborne song "Blood

On Risers". I have to admit that for a split minute I was scared and I didn't know what I had gotten in to. Throughout jump school I hated to hear that song about a paratrooper who forgot to hook up his static line and fell to his death. As dawn finally came, I could see who was making all of that noise running. There were hundred of guys just like me all over the place lining up getting ready for training. Jump school is three weeks long. You have to run everywhere. If you are caught walking you have to drop and do twenty push-ups. In jump school rank didn't matter. I saw a sergeant make a captain get down and do twenty push-ups. First you were broken down into different platoon size classes. Then each class had to give its class number and motto every day. I was in Airborne Class #33, "Good To The Last Drop". I made it up and everybody liked it. So the training began. Everyday we had to run twenty miles to build up our ankles and legs. Then we did PT (physical training) and ran some more. When it was time to eat, we just shoved the food in our mouths got up and ran out of the mess hall. One soldier ask me what I had just eaten and I couldn't even tell him. You were always kept in a high state of readiness. We always ran to the cadence of " Stand up, Hook up, Shuffle to the door, Jump right out and count to four. If that chute don't open wide, I got another one by my side. During training we learn how to do a PLF (Parachute Landing Fall). We jumped from the forty foot tower and finally from the two hundred and fifty foot tower. To graduate from jump school you have to make five jumps, two on Monday, two on Tuesday and one on Wednesday. We made our jumps from a C-119 and a C141 Jet. When it was time for me to make my jumps I wasn't scared at all just a little apprehensive. The plane took off circled and it was time for the jumpmaster to give the nine jump commands. They are: get ready, outboard personnel stand up, inboard personnel stand up, hook up, check static line, check equipment, sound off for equipment check, stand in the door, go. The line starting moving. I was fifth from the door, then fourth, then third, second and then it was my turn and I just jumped out the door. I counted, one thousand, two thousand, three thousand and I felt my chute pull me back and slow me down. I opened my eyes and saw that I was floating down. The jump was exciting. I enjoyed the ride down. Now it was time to land so I made sure that my legs were together and slightly bent and then I landed. I jumped up and no broken bones. I was happy. I did that four more times and on my fifth jump as I landed a colonel was driving around saying "All The Way" soldier. The colonel would come up to us and pin our wings on our chest and say that we were now paratroopers. He would then shake our hands. From now on when ever we saluted an officer we would say "All The Way, Sir". That had to be the best and happiest day of my life when I got those wings. I still have my blood wings. I was now a shock trooper, a super trooper an airborne trooper. Everybody was happy. We had all graduated from jump school. We all got our paratrooper wings. Now we can wear the glider patch on our hats.

We could also wear jump boot with our dress uniform. The jump boot is the thing that paratroopers are made of. You can steal his car, or take his money but don't mess with his jump boots. The best ones to get were Cocoran. You can tell because on the bottom of the boot near the instep of the boot there would be the letter C. That's how you knew that you had the best boots. You always shined the heel and toe so that you could see your face in them. The shine on the boot tells everyone how much time you spent on your boots. Some of the guys would get a reinforced sole and heel to make the boots look a lot larger than they were. Either way you looked at it a paratrooper would rather die than give up his jump boots and that's a fact. After we got back to the barracks, we were dismissed to clean up and we were given liberty. A lot of us went into Columbus, Georgia to celebrate. You could always tell when new paratroopers were in town fresh from jump school because they always wanted to drink the town dry and fight everyone they see. That's because we were told that we could beat anybody and some of the guys wanted to prove it. The paratrooper way was simple, you would pick a fight with anybody and have them chase you until they got tired then you would turn around and whip their behind. The reason this technique always worked is because everyone knows that paratroopers always run at least twenty miles a day and then start his training. After the beer had been drank and the stories have all been told it was time to go back to Benning to get ready for our new home, wherever that will be. The next morning we stood outside in formation listening to the first sergeant tell us where we will be going. Some of us would be going to Fort Campbell Kentucky home of the 101st Airborne Division, the Screaming Eagles. The rest of us was going to Fort Bragg North Carolina home of the 82nd Airborne Division, the All Americans. I was going to the 82nd.

Fort Bragg

I took the bus and arrived at Fort Bragg at about 10 p.m. I was sent to the replacement company. This is where they send you until they figure out which battalion you will be sent to. After two days I was sent to the third battalion the five oh fourth infantry (3/504). I started my infantry training just like everyone else. The difference is that since this will be unit until I get out of the army I didn't half to get up at four o'clock in the morning. Now it was like a job. You did field training exercises and every so often you made a jump. You had to jump to stay on jump status. On day I was told to go to the company commander's office. When I got there he told me that I had been selected to go to rigger school at Fort Lee, Virginia. A rigger is a person that packs parachutes and also packs other military machines (tanks, jeeps, howitzers etc.) to be dropped from planes. I thought that I might like it so I went. Fort Lee is a very small post. It is a school post. Most people who go there are going to some kind of school. I was given my orientation about being a parachute rigger. I was told that after I finished I would be wearing the red hat of a rigger. I was told that this would be a nine to five type of job. So I went to class, which was held at night starting at eight o'clock and lasting until one in the morning. Already I didn't like it because it wasn't exciting enough for me. You just packed parachutes over and over until you got it right. One parachute was supposed to take a good rigger thirty-five minutes. I stayed in class and decided to continue the class. Around about this time I had met a first sergeant and he said that he had been watching me and that my father must be very proud of me because he could tell that I was every inch a soldier. I told him that I had no father. He then ask me if I had a mother and I said yes but she doesn't really care about me. He just smiled and said that he would like for me to have dinner at his house with him and his wife. I wasn't doing anything special so I went. His wife was a very nice lady and when she answered her door she said that you must be James. I said yes ma'am and she invited me in. We had dinner and after ward we sat down and the first sergeant said that I must be wondering why he ask me over for dinner. I said yes I was. He said James the reason that I ask you over here was because I want to ask you a question. What I want to ask you is would you like to be my son. He said that his wife could not have any children and they are both getting older and that he had no son to carry on. He could see that I was shocked and that I didn't know what to say. He said that if he had a son he would want him to be just like me. A million things were going through my head. I didn't know these people. They seemed genuine. I just didn't know what to say. I told the first sergeant that I would have to think very hard about it. So I thought about it. This was a white guy and his wife. I was a black young man. This was the first time someone had been that straight forward and kind to me to ask me such a thing. This was the first time someone saw me as a person and color didn't matter. This was the first time that someone wanted me for something. However, the dye had been cast. I couldn't do it. I was my own person. I was making it in the world on my own. I was becoming a man. The next day I saw the first sergeant and told him that I really appreciated his offer and that had this been another time and place and I would've accepted it, but that I can't because I have to make it on my own. He just looked at me and said the he told his wife that he doesn't expect me to say yes because he could see that I was trying to stand on my own two feet. He thanked me and told me that if I ever have any problems or wanted anything, and it doesn't matter what it is to just call him. We shook hands and the next day I ask for a transfer back to infantry.

    I had to wait one week for my transfer back to Fort Bragg. Being a rigger was not for me. I was 11B1P an infantry parachutist. I finally got my transfer back to Fort Bragg. The year was 1969. The Vietnam war was heating up pretty fast. The United States was constantly sending troops overseas.

James W. Clark

I was at Fort Bragg with the 3/504th. While I was at Fort Lee, Virginia, the third brigade had made a combat jump into Vietnam. This was the first combat jump that the 82nd had made since World War II. When I returned to Bragg they were reforming the third Brigade again because everyone else had gone to Vietnam. So once again I trained constantly. When there was time I would go into Fayetteville with some of my friends and drink beer and talk to some girls. After a while I was getting tired of training and I requested to see the company commander. I told him that I wanted to 10-49 to Vietnam. A 10-49 means transfer. He ask me if I was sure that's what I wanted to do. I said yes. He told me that there is a levy coming down in about a month and he will make sure that my name was on it. He ask me why I wanted to go to Vietnam. I told him that I was tired of training and that I wanted to do it for real and I wasn't worried about dying. He just said ok you got it.

Chapter 12

Home, On Leave

I RECEIVED A THIRTY DAY LEAVE IN APRIL 1969. I TOOK THE BUS FROM Fayetteville North Carolina all the way to Pittsburgh, PA. I went to see my girlfriend and we partied everyday with our friends. I went to see my mother to let her know that I was going to Vietnam and the first thing that she said was don't forget to sign your insurance over to me before you go over seas. I told her that I didn't have to sign it over to her and that I had signed it over to Virginia. My mother hit the roof. She called me every dirty name that she could think of. She told me that I wasn't any son to her because if I was I would sign the insurance over to her and that she hoped that I got killed. I didn't say anything to her. There was nothing to say. I saw the whole picture now. She was hoping that I got killed just so that she could collect the $10k that the beneficiary was given when someone in the service was killed. I just walked away and didn't say anything. I thought that was the end of it. Two day before I was to leave I had to go out to Oakdale army base to pick-up my travel tickets. I was waiting for a bus back to Pittsburgh when this officer picked me up and gave me a ride. We started talking and he was very impressed with my uniform. I was dressed in my dressed greens with the blue infantry rope on one arm and the red and green French rope on the other arm. I had my PFC stripe on. I had my ninety day ribbon and blue unit citation, my expert rifle badge and my jump wings on my left breast pocket, I had my glider cap on and my jump boots were shining like glass. I was STRAC (Strategtic Touch Ready And Combative). This officer started telling me why he never went Airborne. What it boil down to was that he was scared of the training that paratroopers and rangers go through and he felt that he wasn't tough enough to join. I just said that its never to late to join. He just said that if they all looked like you then our country is in good hands.

We both had a good laugh. While driving and talking he happen to look at my name plate and said is your last name Clark and I said yes sir. Then he proceeded to tell me about a woman named Mary Clark that went down to the federal building in downtown Pittsburgh and told the people at the army recruiter station that I was AWOL and that she wanted me picked up. They kept telling her that they can't do anything until they get orders. The officer told me that she persisted and started causing a scene to the point that they had to have four MPs throw her out. They told her that if she came back then they would arrest her. I told the officer that she was my mother. I was so ashamed to hear him tell me something like that, that I just wanted to jump out of the car and just walk back to the city. I was completely embarrassed. I told the officer that I was not AWOL, that I was on my way to Vietnam and that I had went to Oakdale to get my travel orders and ticket. He said that he understood and he hopes that I make it back. Obviously my mother would try to do anything to get me in trouble because I didn't sign my insurance over to her.

After saying my good-byes the next day, I got on the greyhound bus heading for Fort Lewis Washington. The trip took three days. When I arrived at the bus station I was hungry. I didn't have any money but a very kind gentleman offered to buy me breakfast if I would have just one drink with him. Of course I agreed. I informed him that I was on my way to Vietnam. He said that he kind of knew that and the purpose of the drink is to wish me well. I thanked him for it and sat down and had a very large breakfast. He let me get as much as I could eat. I shook his hand and caught a bus to Fort Lewis Washington. Once again I was sent to a replacement company until the next day. The next day we were all taken to these giant warehouses. In these warehouses were clothes and all type of gear for jungle fighting. Other warehouses were stocked with gear for fighting in snow or other extreme cold weather. We received our jungle fatigues, jungle boots and insect repellant. We received water purification tablets, canteens and our rucksacks. We had received all of our shots and now we were ready to board the Braniff Airline jet for the eighteen hour flight to Vietnam.

Chapter 13

Vietnam 1969 – 1970, Smitty

THE FLIGHT WAS LONG AND BORING. EVERYONE WAS JOKING AND PLAYING around and no one seem bothered by the fact that we are on our way to war. It seem like a fun trip. When we arrived over southeast Asia it was dark. Someone said "look you can see the tracers". As I looked out of the window I could see the tracers flying back and forth. That was an indication that someone was doing a lot of fighting. We landed at Ton Son Nuht Air base in South Vietnam. As soon as we stepped off of the plane the air was stifling. It was very hot and it was almost after mid-night. We were put into barracks and told that we would be shipped out tomorrow.

The next day at around eight o'clock the temperature was already over one hundred and five degrees. It was going to be hot and humid. We stood in formation and waited for our name to be called telling us where we would be going. I heard my name and I found out that I was going to the 173rd Airborne Brigade which was located at LZ North English. But first I had to go to jungle school in Charang Valley. Here they break you in. This is where they let you know that this is real war and people do get killed. They show you the different booby traps like the bouncing betty, or the punji stakes. The tell you to be on the lookout for sappers. These guys will spend one hour to crawl six feet just to either kill you or set a booby trap. I stayed at Charang Valley for about three days then it was on to Binh Dinh Providence, Tam Quan District. I was put on a Huey helicopter and flown to LZ English. There was six of us on the Huey and I was the only one going to LZ North English. The rest were staying at LZ English. A couple of the guys that were staying at LZ English were going to the 75th Rangers. There were many different Ranger Battalions but from what I know, November 75th was the one that you wanted to get in to. They were hard core. I got me a ride to North

James W. Clark

English in a jeep. LZ North English was about five miles up the road just off of highway 1. There were four companies there. I was assigned to company E 4/503rd. Our barracks were right next to the berm where the 105 howitzers were. When they had a fire mission those guns would shake the barracks and give me a headache all night long. The next day I was given some insect repellant, C rations, water and ammunition. I was given about four bandoliers of ammo for my M-16, grenades, claymore mines, white phosphorous grenades (willy pete) a couple of M72 laws and machine gun ammo. After that me and another trooper were sent to the field. To also confirm what I already knew was real, while we were sitting at the heliport waiting for a Huey to pick us up there was a commotion in the village. Since the village was only about fifty meters my friend and I went over to check things out. We were new in country and new to the ways of the war. When we got to the village we found out that the hamlet chief had just been shot and that they were searching everyone looking for the person and the weapon. The Quan Camh (National Police) had arrived and was questioning and searching everyone. Because of our culture differences the women knew that Americans were not going to actually touch them or look down their blouses so the National Police search them while the Americans search the men. As it turned out they found a fifteen year old girl who had shot the hamlet chief. The weapon that she used was a 38 special. After the shooting she tied a piece of string to the weapon and let it hang down between her legs and the other end she put around her neck and you couldn't tell that she had anything. I have to give it to the National Police, these guys are worse than the Gestapo. When they ask you a question you had better give them an answer. I saw them take this girl over by one of the jeeps and beat her up. But she wouldn't talk. They kept pounding on her and she wouldn't tell them anything. Finally they tore her clothes off of her and tied her to the jeeps. Her arms were tied to one jeep and her legs were tied to the other one. They gave her one more chance to talk and when she didn't they just started up the jeeps and pulled her apart. After that they gave the rest of the villagers a stern warning about helping the Vietcong or the NVA and then they left. My friend and I went back to the heliport and thought about what we had saw. That was our indoctrination into the real war. A Huey came and took us to our platoon out in the jungle. It was getting dark. My first night in country in the bush. The Huey dropped us off and left just that quick. I notice that a lot of troopers came up to the helicopter to unload the supplies and took my friend with them. I just stood there not knowing where to go or what to do. This guy came up to me and shook my hand and said that his name was Smitty. He said that it was sure nice to have another brother in the platoon. For the short time that I knew Smitty he showed me a lot. The first thing that he told me was that the platoon was full of rednecks and they don't like black guys. Smitty told me that he feels that they had been trying to get him killed and that we should watch each others back. I agreed. He told me to always take an extra bandolier of ammo with me no matter where I went and don't panic if I'm left out in the jungle by myself. We kind of stayed close for a few days. I could see that Smitty was for real. I had a couple rednecks tell me that I had better stay in my place while I'm in the platoon. I told them that they're the ones that had better stay in their place. Smitty came back and told me that word had gotten around that I wasn't afraid of them and that they couldn't scare me so they don't know what to think at this point. Smitty was short (ready to go home soon). He had no business staying in the field. He showed me pictures of his twin daughters that his wife had. He was going home in a week. Usually when you're short you go to the rear to start getting ready to leave but someone didn't want Smitty to leave the field. Smitty was sent on an ambush three days before he was to leave. When the patrol came back Smitty was the only one killed. I was told that a gook jumped up in front of him and shot him and ran away. I found that hard to believe. Rodriguez started saying how much do (marijuana) and money that he had taken off of Smitty's body. I knew that Smitty was killed and I don't know why or what for. All that I know is that Smitty like myself was black and everybody else in the platoon was white. I couldn't prove anything because I wasn't on the patrol. He was just another KIA. After that happened I started sleeping during the day when I could. That allowed me to stay up all night. I was becoming pretty good at moving around in the jungle and walking point. I foiled a couple of ambushes because I was paying attention to what I was doing. I was given the nickname "The Liquidator". I was even given a "drive-on" rag with that on it. The guys in the platoon started getting very scared of me because I had learned to become a good jungle fighter and so far I had four personal kills. These guys wanted to go home. When you want to go home you start getting scared that you won't make it. The white boys were starting to get freaked out because to them I was strange. Personally I really didn't care if I went home or not. I didn't have any one waiting for me. My family has been dispersed for years and as far as I was concerned to me this was home. The white boys started trying to become my friend. They were fake. They were just scared that I would throw a grenade in their tent at night. They knew that I always roamed around at night. As soon as the sun went down all you heard was where's Clark. I volunteered for night patrol just to get away from those guys. I felt safer in the jungle than I did with them.

First Time Wounded
Brothers & Reese

The color of the platoon started changing. We started getting more brothers in the platoon. Some of the white guys had gotten killed in ambushes and some of them went home. The ones that were left, all of a sudden they wanted to be your good buddy. But I remembered Smitty. The guys that were coming into the platoon were from New York, Baltimore, Philly and LA. These guys were sure nuff brothers. We had another white guy come to the platoon. His name was Reese. He was a big white boy with curly blond hair and he looked like he played football. He was our new machine gunner. He was put into my squad. He didn't stay off by himself he kind of gravitated towards all of the brothers. I started talking to him and I found out that he was from Kentucky. He told me something and to this day I find it hard to believe. What he told me was that he had never seen a black person before. He said that he had seen them on television but he thought that people had painted theirselves like that. When he joined the army he couldn't believe what he was seeing. Hell, I couldn't believe what I was hearing. After all this was 1969. I told a couple of my friends and they couldn't believe it either. We all kept asking Reese just how far back in the hills did he live in Kentucky. What a laugh. Anyway Reese hung with the brothers all of the time and a lot of the white boys resented it. They started asking Reese what's he doing hanging with those niggers. Of course there were fights. Reese and I started getting tight because we always went out on patrol together and we always went out on ambushes together. After a while people would say Clark where is your shadow. Once Reese and I stopped a rape that was about to happen. We were in this village just walking around and we saw a circle of people so we went over to investigate. What we saw was to of the rednecks that were in our platoon getting ready to rape this little girl in front of her parents. I asked them what did they think they were doing. One of them said what does it look like. I just said well its not going to happen today. After I said that they picked up their M-16s as though they were going to shoot me. They also had a couple more friends with them and told us to leave if we know what's good for us. At this time three of my partners came around one of the hooches and saw what was about to happen and at that moment there was a standoff. Me, Reese Sugar Bear, Carter and Wild E against five rednecks. They backed down and left. The father and mother were very happy and they thanked us with food and soda. None of us could understand why did they have to rape someone when there are girls in Tam Quan for that purpose. In any event we kept running patrols and ambushes. On one ambush, we didn't get set up quick enough and some Vietcong were coming down the trail. One of them saw me at the same time that I saw him. We both froze, and then he threw a grenade. It exploded and a small piece hit me on my chest bone just below my neck. That was July 1969. I was medivac out to the rear. They took a very small piece of shrapnel out and I was on R&R for about four days. Later on I came back to the platoon. I found out while I was in the rear that we were fighting the 96th North Vietnamese Army (NVA Yellowstar). The difference between the NVA and the Vietcong is that the NVA is well trained and come down from the north and will stay and fight it out with you to the last man. The

Vietcong would use hit and run tactics. Once we were supposed to go and reinforce a platoon of South Vietnamese army regulars. There were about fifty of them and there were only eight of us. When the sun goes down the moon comes out after 2 am. Between that time it is pitch black and that's when the attacks began. You could hear the NVA and the Vietcong shouting "G.I. you die tonight". Then they started blowing the bugles and finally the B-40 rockets started coming. The main part of the attack was on the ARVN side. When they attacked our side they knew that we weren't going to run away. Some of the ARVNs stayed and fought. The others ran away. One ARVN was trying to hide underneath me. I got mad and told him to start shooting. I could see that he was scared and didn't want to fight. I just kicked him out of the way and kept on fighting. The NVA kept on coming and at first I thought that I was missing them. But I could see my tracers going right through them and I couldn't figure out why they kept on coming. Then I heard Reese say that they must be high on liquid OJ's (liquid opium joints) and to shoot them in the head. So that's what we did. We took them off at the neck and the body would keep coming for a few long seconds then drop. That battle lasted all night long. The next morning there were bodies all over the place. The ARVN that wouldn't fight was killed also. There were helicopters coming in from all over the place. There were soldiers coming in to relieve us. We were tired from fighting all night but we were happy to see the sun come up. The Brigade commander arrived to tell us that we had done a good job. No kidding. Reese and I decided to have our self some breakfast of cocoa and beef and rice lrrp (long range recon patrol meals) and just watch the activity going on. After all of the activity had died down our squad started the one click back to the platoon (one click equals 1000 meters). Our platoon was located on a hill along side of highway one. We usually launched our ambushes and just regular patrols from this location. Sometimes we would go on a CA (Combat Assault) in which helicopters would come and pick us up and drop us right in the middle of a hot LZ (Landing Zone).

Sniper's Island
Second Time Wounded

The time now is November and we were on our way to Snipers Island. It wasn't really an island, its just that this place is surrounded by rice paddies full of water and it was very large and wide. A lot of NVA were hiding out there and every time some of our troops went there some one got killed or wounded. There was a lot of elephant grass that had fallen over and people could hide under it. The elephant grass grows to about six feet or more in height. After we landed we started our search and destroy mission. We had walked for about fifteen minutes when the firing started. Someone was shooting at us. We traded shots for about twenty minutes and the firing died down. We were finding the enemy laying under the elephant grass just as we thought. As I walked away I heard a rustle of grass and as I turned I saw this person throw a chi com (Chinese Communist) grenade at me. My partner and I dove at the same time and then there was an explosion. I felt pain in my left foot. It felt like it had been blown off. I was more afraid that the NVA soldier that threw the grenade was coming to make sure that we were dead. So I rolled left and my partner roll right so that if he was coming he would have two targets and one of us would get him. I didn't want to wait, my foot was hurting and swelling up and the pain drove me to action. I went forward through the grass and I saw him laying there breathing hard. I emptied my whole magazine just to make sure that he was dead. Afterward, I found out that he was a fourteen-year-old boy. I did not feel any remorse. I figured that if he was old enough to pick up a rifle and shoot someone, he was old enough to get shot. I was nineteen.

Qui Nhon Hospital 67th Evac

The dustoff came (medical helicopters) and took me to a field hospital. They immediately cut all of my clothes off and had to pry my fingers from my M-16. I did not want to let go of my weapon. I had become very proficient with my M-16. I did not have to aim in order to hit my target. Just like a gunfighter of the old west, all that I had to do was look at where I wanted the bullet to go and shoot from the hip. I always hit my target. Eye and hand coordination, (it really works). I was counting backwards from one hundred until I was knocked out. The funny thing is that I could still feel them cutting on me. When I woke up I was in the 67 Evac Hospital in Qui Nhon. My foot was throbbing and they had used some wire to close the wound. The hospital ward was full of guys from the 101st, 1st Cav and the 173rd. The other half of the ward was filled with guys from the South Vietnamese army. There was a bed that was three away from mine with a partition around it. On the third day they removed the partition and I saw the guy laying in the bed. He was a lieutenant and he had both of his arms and legs blown off and he was happy to be alive. I guess my wounds didn't seem so serious after looking at him. I got a visit from General Barns, the Brigade Commander. They always come around and give you a pep talk that really doesn't amount to much. So you just listen and are happy when they leave. I was happy like everyone else because it was Thanksgiving and that means turkey, cranberry sauce, stuffing, pie and some pop to drink. I never thought that I would get so much food in the hospital. At the same time the orderlies came to move me to the runway to go to Cam Rahn Bay. I started putting up a fuss telling them that I wasn't going until I finish my food. The nurses come in and told them to send me on the next flight in a couple of days. I enjoyed all of my food that day. That night I slept good. In the early morning I woke up cold and shivering. I didn't know why. I know that the ward did not have air-conditioning but I was very cold and when I put my hand under the blankets everything felt wet. I could not believe that I had urinated on myself, but I was wet all over. The best way to describe what I saw is to say that it was just like the part in the Godfather movie when the guy throws the cover back and there is blood all over the place (minus the horse head). I was red from the waist down. I had been laying in my blood so long that it had soaked through the mattress and started a medium size puddle under my bed. The blood was thick like pudding. A little Vietnamese lady came by my bed and just shook her head. She thought that I was on my way out. I started hollering for a nurse and one finally came. She gasped when she saw all of the blood. I guess she thought that a wound had opened up or something. In any event I got a blood transfusion and after a couple of days I was moved to Cam Ranh Bay to heal up. I stayed there about five weeks and was sent back to my unit at LZ North English.

An Incident At LZ North English

I was not sent back to the field for at least a month. Instead I was given the company truck to drive around in and make deliveries. I took hot food to the guys on the bridge and to other units that weren't so far in the bush. Every time I went past this village I always gave them the extra food. I figured no since in throwing it away. No only that, but each time before I left the LZ I would always check the kitchen to see if they had any extra food that they were going to throw away and I would get it by saying that I was going to give it to the guys in the field. The guys in the field could only eat so much so I would give it to some of the poor villagers and they were very happy to get it. After the cooks found out what I was doing with the extra food they got mad and wouldn't give me any more leftovers. I think that was because they wanted to sell it. Anyway my driving days were over and I was back in the field again. The monsoon had come. It was winter. I rained all of the time. These raindrops were big and they hurt when they hit your face. There was no since in trying to stay dry. Not only that, but the humidity was terrible. The temperature would be one hundred and ten degrees and it would be raining hard. There were many things about living in the jungle that you needed to know. One of them was your senses became very sharp. You don't need to wear sun glasses in the bush. You needed to see whats in front of you and not enjoy the pretty colors. Your nose became very sensitive. You could smell whether or not someone was just there in that area. Above all, when you wash up you do not use ivory soap or any soap for that matter. Americans have a habit of using soap when bathing and not only that, but Americans like to put on after shave lotions and cocoa butter to smell good. These things are a definite No, No. When washing in the jungle you just use plain old water to wipe down with. Its best not to wear new jungle clothes because they have a new smell to them. Its also best not to wear new boots because the creak when you wear them and they smell new to. Also you never ever use cologne, shaving cream, cocoa butter or anything that will give off a scent. The enemy can smell you as well as you can smell them. I traded all of my new stuff in for used items. An incident happened when I went to the rear for clothes and a hot meal. One of the food servers and I got into it about the food. The food servers were Vietnamese. I ask her for more cake and she refused to give it to me so I took a piece. She hit me on my hand with a cooking ladle. I reached over the counter to back hand her and instead hit a pot of lemon sauce. It fell over and the lemon sauce spilled over and some of it got on her and burned her. By that time I had gotten an extra piece of cake and chicken and was in the mess hall eating. The sergeant major came in cussing and said where is that son of a bitch that knocked over that pot on that girl. Everybody pointed to me. He came over mad and red in the face and since he was armed with a forty-five he saw me put my hand on the trigger of my M-16 and that calmed him down. He ask me why did I do it and I said that it was an accident and that I didn't know that the sauce was hot. He just said to come over to his office after I finished eating and that we would talk about it. After I got over to his office I was arrested and told that I would be going to Long Binh Stockade. I also found out that he told the girls involved that I was going to be punished because as a black soldier I should know better and that they know how to deal with black people in the U.S..

Chapter 14

The Shocking Revelation of the U.S. Army Comradeship

So I was sent to the Long Binh Stockade in the south. When I first got there they put me what was called a conex. Basically it was a dumpster with one side cut off and bars put on. Naturally with the heat there it was like an oven. One of the guards was nice enough to let us out almost all day because it was just too hot to be in a cage. The next day a white guard came and unlocked my cell and said something to me about teaching me a lesson. We started to fight and I beat him up. He crawled out of the cell very quickly and left. I thought that was the end of that but it wasn't. He came back with four other white guards and they jumped me in my cell. Only because there were more of them, I got beat up and they even handcuffed me to the bars and worked me over, you know, kicking me between the legs, kicking me in my stomach and punching me. Afterwards they uncuffed me and I fell to the floor of the cell. When they were leaving I heard one of them say that should teach that nigger a lesson. Right there, I changed my mind about becoming a thirty-year man. One of my heroes was Sgt. Rock of Easy Company. I use to always buy his comic books. Sgt Rock was a thirty-year man and I had already made up my mind to stay in the army for thirty years. Another guy that I liked was a staff sergeant named Charles E. Williams, alias Charlie E. He was already a thirty-year man and his favorite line was "I'm going to stay in the army until the army turns navy and them I'm going to re-up (re-enlist) for six more". Charles E Williams was from Louisiana. He had fifteen children and he always made sure that his wife was pregnant. He was in World War II and the Korean War. He knew a lot of tricks about jungle fighting and a lot of grunts liked him. I had just decided that I didn't want to stay in an army where you travel ten thousand miles to fight and you're still thought of as a nigger and not a soldier. I found out that later they wanted to beat me to death but an American soldier was beaten to death in the stockade and that there was a congressional investigation and that the stockade could not afford any more deaths like that one. I was put in solitary confinement for two weeks. I was actually given bread and water. I was given two slices of bread and all of the water that I wanted (I thought that they only did that in the movies). While there I contracted hepatitis. There was no A or B but then, just hepatitis. I didn't know that I had it. All that I know is that I was sick and my food was not staying down. Some one told me to ask the guard if I could go to the bathroom. Once there I was told to check my urine to see if it was black. I ask the guard if I could go to the bathroom and he came down and let me out of my cell. When I got to the bathroom I started to urinate. I was shock at what was coming out of me. The fluid that was coming out of me was black as ink. All that I could think of was "I got it". I told the guard and he said that I would have to go to the hospital. When he took me back to my cell, I ask him if I could thank the guy in the next cell for telling me what to look for. The guard looked puzzled and said that I was the only one there and that everyone else had been moved two weeks ago. I said if that's true, then who was I talking to. We both just shrugged our shoulders. The next day two guards came to get me to take me to the hospital. I was very sick and weak. I couldn't stand up and they kept yelling for me to stand up but I couldn't. They drugged me out of my cell and were dragging me down the road when a jeep pulled up and the officer ask them why they were dragging me. They said that I was a prisoner and because I was too sick to stand up. The officer told them that I was still an American soldier and to pick me up and carry me. They did but when they got to the hospital they just threw me down and left. What I found out about hepatitis is that your liver is infected and your urine turns black and you cannot eat. Any little thing you try to eat your body throws it back up. Later your skin turns real yellow. This is the jaundice. Your eyes also turn yellow. They didn't give me any medicine, they just told me to keep trying to eat something until some of the food starts to stay down. That is a sign that you are getting better. To get rid of the hepatitis takes about two months and slowly the yellow disappears and your urine turns back to a light yellow. After I got better I was sent to the stockade and waited for my trial.

Chapter 15

The Court-Martial

MY TRIAL WAS A SPECIAL COURT-MARTIAL. THE WITNESSES THAT WERE called against me were the mess hall cooks and the first sergeant. They all said that the girls never bad mouth the soldiers and were always polite. They said that I was complaining because I wasn't given enough food and since I was mad, that I picked the hot pot of lemon sauce up over my head and dumped it on the girls (a lie). The first sergeant basically said the same thing. My lawyer was pretty good. He ask the questions that needed to be ask. For example, was the girl in question his girlfriend? The first sergeant said no (a lie). Did he tell the girls and their parents that he knows how to deal with blacks when they get out of line at home and that I will be dealt with. Again the first sergeant said no (a lie). My lawyer also ask him if he said that black soldiers are always causing trouble and the army is trying to do something about. Once again the first sergeant said no (a lie). Finally my lawyer ask him to demonstrate just how I picked the pot up. The first sergeant showed the court with another pot how I picked the pot up over my head and doused the girl with lemon sauce. My lawyer then asks him if the lemon sauce was hot and he replied that he didn't know. He did say that lemon sauce was usually hot though. My lawyer then stated to the court that if I had done what these people stated, then my hands would be burned. I had to stand up and show my hands, which obviously weren't burned. The court recessed and when they returned I was given a reduction in rank and fined two hundred and fifty dollars and given timed served with a suspended sentence. I was on my way home.

Deros (Going Home)

I was sent back to my unit at LZ North English in Bong Son. I started to prepare for leaving Vietnam. I had to turn in my equipment and get a lot of paper work filled out. I went to Battalion headquarters for my reenlistment pep talk. If I signed up for another six years, I would get ten thousand dollars. I explained to the reenlistment officer what had happened to me and I told him that this is not the type of army that I wanted to be in. He said that he understood and after I signed my papers, he wished me good luck. The flight that I came back home on was Braniff Airlines. I was very happy when the pilot said that we had reached the continental U.S. and that we would be landing at Fort Lewis Washington. After landing, all that I wanted to do was take a hot shower and drink me a Pepsi. I was mustered out of the army on 5 August 1970. I had two hundred and fifty dollars in cash and two cheques for a total of thirty five hundred dollars. I put the two cheques inside my shirt and I was given a ride to the Seattle Airport where I brought a one way ticket to Pittsburgh Penna. I flew on Eastern Airlines.

Chapter 16

Back in the World

ONCE AGAIN I ARRIVED IN PITTSBURGH AT NIGHT. NO ONE KNEW THAT I was home. I went to my girlfriend's house and we hooked up and went out to party. We got us an apartment and I brought me a 1965 white Buick Rivera. The fifth night that I was home the police stopped me and they found out that I didn't have a regular driving license just a military license so I was arrested and taken downtown to the Number 1 police station. I was in the holding cell when a detective came over and ask me if I'd mind standing in a lineup. I told him that I didn't mind. He ask me what was I in for and I told him driving without a license and that I had just returned home about five days ago from Vietnam. He said that if that's true then say something to me in Vietnamese. I did, and he said that it sounds like greek to him and that he would speak to the judge for me. When it was my turn to go before the judge, he ask me if I had just come home. I said yes sir. He said that he liked boys who served their country and for me to go home. When I got out my girlfriend was waiting for me. She told me that some bondsman was trying to get her to sleep with him and that if she did, he would get me out of jail. He didn't know that the judge had already freed me. So when he came up he acted like he had gotten me out and that I owed him something. I told him that I didn't owe him nothing and to get out of my face. He just left. I ask my girlfriend if she had given him any money and she said no. My girlfriend and I got on with our lives. We moved from the Hill to Oakland. Oakland was a pretty nice place to live. The University of Pittsburgh was there. That part of Pittsburgh was strictly University and Medical centers. Oakland was a lot more quiet than the Hill District.

James W. Clark

Settling Down In The World

I got a job as a furniture refinisher. I used the GI benefits to help me. The government paid for my training as a furniture refinisher while I was working. Not only that, but the state of Pennsylvania paid me two hundred dollars for going to Vietnam. Also I was a disabled vet with 10% disability. Back then the 10% was only twenty three dollars. So we lived kind of comfortable. The year was 1970. We drove my car all of the way down to Beeville Texas to see some friends. By that time I had brought another Buick Rivera, a 1973. It was a very nice looking and fast car. We drove to Washington, D.C. and to Niagara Falls, Canada. I took us everywhere. In 1973 we moved from Oakland to Northview Heights. These were projects. A lot of the people in these projects were on welfare and did not work. They would sleep until four o'clock in the afternoon and stay up all night. I was one of the ones that got up and went to work everyday. On the weekends, I drank Iron City beer and Canadian Club whiskey. We always went to the Hill to the bars to party until the bars close then we would go and get some fish. On Sunday I would take my girlfriend to church and I would sleep the rest of the day. Things weren't too bad. I had people (friends) calling me, wanting me to hang out with them. But these people didn't work and I did and I knew that I needed to get up on Monday morning and go to work. I even got another job downtown at this new restaurant, washing dishes. I didn't mind doing dishes and besides at the end of the evening they would always allow us to take home food that they were going to throw away. I couldn't believe the amount of food that was being thrown away. They were throwing away whole chickens, racks of lamb, large deep-sea shrimp, pounds of sausages many different kinds of dessert. So I was very happy that they allowed us to take some of the food home. We ate very well for awhile. I decided to quit that job because I wasn't getting any sleep and I needed to concentrate on my graining technique on furniture. I continued to work at the furniture store, all the while I kept getting the feeling that I should be some where else. I worked on that job for three years. I learned the art of graining furniture, antiquing furniture also repairing furniture. I worked on a lot of Drexel Heritage furniture and Hibriten furniture. However I kept on feeling that I should be somewhere else. So I told my girlfriend that we are going to be moving to California. She didn't want to go. She suggested that we just move somewhere else in Pittsburgh. I told her that I needed to go somewhere that pays a lot more money and have more opportunities for a black person. She bucked and kicked at every chance about not wanting to go with me. I told her that I would go first and come back to get her when I found a good job. She didn't say anything. I paid the rent for three months and left her some money to live on and then I left.

My Journey To L.A.

I got as far as Effingham Illinois when my car broke down. This was decision time. I could turn around and go back, (in which I knew what was back there and I would be stuck doing the same thing) or I could take my clothes out of my car and keep on going west. I decided to keep on going west. I brought me a one way ticket to San Francisco, California. I left my car at the bus station and kept going. On my way to San Francisco I talked to a lot of people on the bus and they basically all said that they think that I would have the best chance of getting what I want in Los Angeles. I still wasn't sure yet. Finally after two days the greyhound pulled into Los Angeles where I was supposed to change buses to go on to San Francisco. A funny thing happened, when the bus driver looked at my ticket, he ask me if I was going there to live and I said yes. He then said that I would have a better chance of making it in LA. That did it. I decided to stay in LA. I had gotten too many omens saying stay in LA. Besides I did have an address of some friends who was supposed to have known my family and had lived in Pittsburgh before moving to LA. I decided to stay at a holiday inn in downtown LA. I didn't know anyone so I took a hot bath and had room service bring me supper and breakfast. I just decided to enjoy myself for this one night before starting out to find these friends the next day. The next day I got up and ate a good breakfast and had a cab take me to the Veterans Administration in Westwood. I figured that these people could help me find a job here in LA. After arriving and talking to a VA representative, it became apparent to me that all that I got was lip service. They will tell you where you can go to apply for a job but they won't call the job site for you. At least they did call for you in Pittsburgh in order to save you time. Also they give you a map of the city and point you in the right direction and say go there. Los Angeles is a very large city. You need a car to get around. I did not have one. Even if you take the bus the ride is pretty long. I decided to find these friends first instead of looking for a job. After all, I did need a place to sleep. I made a couple of phone calls and found that these friends lived in Venice, California. I had enough money for cab fair to take me to Venice. These friends were very nice and were happy to see some one from Pittsburgh out here just like they were. They explained the dynamics of the city and told me the best place to look for work. They told me to try to get a job near a bus line. I rested the whole weekend and put my thoughts in order for the coming Monday. The place that the VA was sending me to was in the San Fernando Valley and that was out of the question for me. I decided to go to the unemployment office in Santa Monica. The lady that helped me was very nice and the first thing that she ask me was did I have a car. I said no. She said that she will try to keep me near a bus line. She told me that she knows how it is to be without a car. The first place she sent me was to a building on Lincoln Boulevard in Santa Monica where the

Greyhound Bus Company was taking applications and giving written test. I filled out my application and was told to return the next day for my test. I felt good. At least this is a start. I didn't want to stay in my friends house no longer than I had to. She was an older woman and her children were my age or older. They came over to visit a lot and we talked about the Steel City and how we wished that we could get some Iron City Beer out here. They did know my family and my family knew them, but they have never seen me before. I guess because I was always living in a foster home and when I grew up I went into the Job Corps then the army. Any way we did a lot of reminiscing about the Steel City and the bottom line was that everyone was glad that they left. They were amazed just like I was that the alleys were so clean and that they sold liquor in the supermarkets. Also the types of housing that they called projects out here were really different from Pittsburgh. The projects out here looked like town houses and they had palm trees and some had swimming pools in them. We all laughed at the difference, especially when we heard someone say that the housing was very bad. We figured that these people don't know how good they have it out here.

Monday I was up early, around 6:00 am and I was out the door by 6:30am. I was in a hurry to get my new life started. I took the blue Santa Monica bus from Venice into Santa Monica over on Lincoln Boulevard. I was mentally prepared to take a test. There were about forty people at the test site. Some were dressed in business suits others were dressed in jeans. I had on a pair of black pants and a white shirt, the only one that I had. To me the test was very easy. You had to know the meaning of about fifty words and then there was a reading and comprehension part. The test was timed. They gave you one and a half hours to complete the test. I took my time. After the time was up, the proctor stated that when he called your name, that meant that you had failed and that you could leave. He began calling out names and people started leaving. Finally there were only me and another person left. The proctor told us that we both passed and we shook each other's hand. The other person left before I did. I was ready to leave when the proctor called me up to his desk. He was a black man in his early fifties. He told me that he was very happy to see that a black man such as myself was able to pass this test. There were only three blacks guys there out of the forty that came to take the test. The proctor ask me if I saw all of those white guys in the business suits and the attaché cases and all of the women in business suits trying to look smart. I said yes. He said that as you know, they all didn't pass the test and that I came dressed in slacks and passed and for my information my score was higher than the white guy that passed with me. This proctor was from the old school. It doesn't matter what you wear as long as you got what's necessary in your head. He told me that if it was up to him he would give me the job today but that this was a weeding out process and that I have passed the first hurdle and to wait until I get a letter from Greyhound. I felt proud for representing the black race in the way that I did. The letter never came. I didn't sit down and wait. I went out the next day on a job interview at a wheel chair company. The name of the company was Everst & Jennnings. I was a frame truer. It was my job to may sure that the frames were straight. The job paid three dollars and twenty five cents an hour. I figure that some money was better than no money. When I got my first pay I gave fifty dollars to the lady that I was staying with. That was the best that I could do. In the mean time I took the Postal Exam test and I went out on a couple more interviews. I was hungry for work. In the mean time I decided to move in with my friends daughter. She had two kids and her apartment was very large and besides I just didn't feel right staying in someone else's mother's house. Also while I was in Pittsburgh, I had started taking up martial arts. I started looking into a school out here to continue my training.

Chapter 17

Tae Kwon Do

LOYALTY, RESPECT, DETERMINATION, FIGHTING SPIRIT. THESE WORDS are the code that I have lived by for more than twenty years. The school that I found was in West LA and it was called Cho's Tae Kwon Do on Santa Monica Boulevard. I liked the school and I liked Master Cho's way of teaching. Now I had somewhere to go after work and something to do. I trained five nights a week and I stayed with Master Cho until I became a second degree blackbelt and he also gave me my instructor's certification. I really enjoyed it. There was a lot of sweat and soreness while learning this art. I would go to practice three times a week and three hours extra on Saturday and about five hours on Sunday. I was even privileged to fight full contact on television on PKA. There were times when Master Cho couldn't teach the class and he would ask me to take over for him. I became a fixture at his school. Master Cho always held his tournaments at the Beverly Hills High School Gym. I was always there in some capacity as either judge or a contestant. I would win some fights and I would lose some fights but you always learned a lot at these tournaments. After a number of years of training, I started breaking bricks. I started with two two inch bricks and went up to five two inch bricks. I started moving up in rank and finally made brown belt. I went to all of Master Cho's tournaments and I also fought in them too. From the training with Master Cho I received my first degree and second degree black belt. I also received my instructors certification from Master Cho's school. Eventually when I moved up to Victorville I was given a chance to open my Tae Kwon Do school. The city of Victorville gave me a building to use for my school. The name of my school was J. Clark's Tae Kwon Do. At first I had only four students because some of the parents thought that I was too strict on the children. But then I got a new crop of students and their parents liked the discipline that I was instilling in their children. My class blew to thirty five children and fifteen adults. I was becoming a household word in Victorville. The year was 1975 and I finally got the call to go and work in the Santa Monica Post Office. My pay rate was seven dollars and twenty two cents per hour. I worked twelve hours a day and I worked all of the time. Once I even stayed on the job for three days before the postal union representative finally told me that I have to go home. Now I was able to save up money and help pay rent where I was staying. After a couple of years I decided to move out into my own apartment. The rent was perfect. It only cost me three hundred dollars a month and it was a one bedroom and I would still be living in Venice. So in the mean time I continue to go to work and workout at Cho's Tae Kwon Do center. In 1978 I decided to quit my job at the Post Office and move back east to Pittsburgh.

CHAPTER 18

My Fearless Attitude: I Will Not Quit

ONCE AGAIN I HAD THAT URGE TO BE IN PITTSBURGH WHEN I WAS ON the west coast. So I left. I thought that I was missing something by not being there, but I wasn't. After I arrived home the first thing that I notice was that nothing has changed. The people that I grew up and went to school with were still doing the same thing. They were still hanging out on the corner and drinking wine and trying to sing doo wop songs. Some of my friends were in Western Penitentiary doing time for robbery or for shooting someone. Also a lot of my friends went to drugs. At that time the drugs were marijuana and heroin, uppers and downers. A lot of people were pill popping every day. These guys still ask me the same thing even after I had been gone for about five years and that is " do I want to get high with them." I told them no and they ask me to buy them a beer which I did. We talked about old times and who is still around and who got killed. The girls that I knew back then, the ones that thought that they were so fine that they wouldn't give me the time of day, they just went to the dogs. Some of them were strung out on H (heroin). Some of them were now prostitutes. Some of them were drunks and still others had let guys beat them up constantly in the name of love, and now they look like battered boxers. A couple of the girls knew me real well and when they saw me they couldn't believe how healthy I was and not all scarred up and smelly. I was polite to them. We went to a bar and I brought them some drinks and we talked about old times. One or two of them even tried to hit on me but we both knew that that was just gaming from the block and nothing was happening. They were looking for money and someone to take them out of the ghetto that they lived in and I had been there and done that. They could've left just like I did but when you're on the streets and you see the fine Eldorado's and Fleetwood Brougham Cadillacs and the silk suits and it seems that everybody has money except you, you can easily fall prey to these trappings of life. You have to look at the big picture and look past the façade that is there in front of you. I left and they stayed. Some of my friends made it and one of my boyhood friends is still there in Pittsburgh. His name is Gunzee. We grew up together, got in fights together, drank wine together and to this day he still calls me to let me know that he is ok. That's my partner. He's a trucker now. I went up to St Clair Village to see a couple of friends of mine and a girl that I hadn't seen for years came up to me to see if I had remembered her. I didn't. I found out later that I had a crush on her and that she was one of the girls that thought that she was too pretty to talk to me. When I saw her she had five children by five different guys and she was looking for an escape. I wasn't it. I never put any of these people down because I grew up there and I understand what it means to live in poverty and what it means to look for something, someone or anything that might be able to help you out. Not everyone can leave and hopefully make somewhere else. I have my path to walk and now even though things are hard for me the people that I've come back to see think that I have it easy and that I've made it. I haven't made it yet. What they see is the result of (so far) hard work and learning. They see that I am my own person and I don't go along with the crowd nor do I go along with anyone just because that person says so. I cannot phone home and ask for help. I cannot even go home because there is none. So I come here because I think that I am missing something but in reality, I am not missing anything. So now I want to go back to the west coast. I have seen that if I would've stayed, I would be like everyone else. Part of me wants to stay and part of me wants to go back to the west coast. I know what it is. Here I have friends and I know the town and I don't really have to struggle to get ahead and of course I was born here. Out west I don't really know the town and do I really want to struggle. I have come to this conclusion. It is better for me to leave Pittsburgh because I can plainly see what I will become by staying here. I will become what I see when I come here to just visit. There are not many good jobs for a black person that would like to get ahead. The steel mills have all closed. Things are changing (very slowly). I don't care who looks the finest or who has the prettiest car. To me its about survival and making it. **I can always come back and be a bum or a wino any time that I get tired of trying**. On the other hand, LA has a lot more to offer. Jobs seem to be plentiful. If you want something and work hard for it, you will get it. Plus I don't have to fight the four month winters out west. So it is to my advantage to go back to LA.

Chapter 19

Los Angeles: Reading, Learning, Studying Opens Successful Doors

I SAID GOOD-BYE TO MY SISTERS AND WAS ON ANOTHER GREYHOUND bus headed for LA. The bus trip took two and a half days which gave me a chance to think. To map out just what I want to do. When I arrived I stayed with some friends in Culver City. The next day immediately got me a job with a travel company. The job was ok and at least I had my own money and I didn't have to ask anyone for anything. While working there I met a girl and we became friends. We would go out to night clubs together. She knew a lot about LA and kind of showed me around. I introduced her to tae kwon do and suggested that she try it. The next time I went to class she came with me and watched the class. She was impressed at how much I knew and the vigorous training. She decided to sign up at Cho's. We became a couple and I moved in with her. Her place was in Los Feliz right next to Hollywood. We went to class together and to tournaments together. Everyone knew us that was in the martial arts circle. She was a very smart woman and she helped me to study and to set up my resume. She always went to Greece and I stayed home to maintain the apartment. We both went to Belize to see a couple of her friends. I like Belize. I found out that there were black people down there whose ancestors were slaves that ran away from the United States and made their home in Central America. Belize is a small Central American country that sit on the east coast of Guatemala. People in that general area spoke with an African dialect. My girlfriend taught me a lot. In the mean time I had gotten a job offer from the IRS office in downtown LA. The job was for a word processor. I had to take the civil service test which I scored an eighty five and I was hired for the job. The job was a step in the right direction but parking downtown was killing me. So I started taking the bus in order to save money. In the mean time my girlfriend decided to move closer to her job in Santa

Monica. We agreed that I should keep the apartment in Los Feliz and she would move to Palms. So sometimes she would stay at my place and other times I would stay at her place. I kept working out on my martial arts because I want to get my first-degree blackbelt. Because of the distance between us we grew apart and we both understood this. We still became very best friends to this day. During this time I decided to go to word processing school because I saw that as a thing of the future. The schools that I looked into all cost a lot of money, and I didn't have enough. I finally found a school that only cost twelve hundred dollars. I figured that I would sell my car for eleven hundred dollars and put one hundred dollars with it and pay the school off. That's exactly what I did. I took the bus to the school everyday until I graduated. The school was a good school in that they had typewriters and they also taught you how to type along with teaching you word processing. What I didn't like about the school was that they always wanted you to pray. I felt that I came to school to learn not to pray and every time they wanted to pray I would just get up and walk out of the classroom until the praying was over. They didn't like it, but I was paying my money. I also felt that they were trying to make me quit because I wasn't going along with their program (when it came to praying.) Their drop out rate was about eighty-five percent. When I started the school there were fifteen people in class. The breakdown was four males and eleven females. All of the guys dropped out except for me and all of the girls dropped out except for five girls. The bottom line was that I was not going to drop out because I had sold my car to pay for this school and I was going to stay and get what I paid for. What I paid for was learning how to type and the understanding of word processing on the Wang System 1140 Computer. When it was time for me to graduate they wanted me to write a graduation speech about what the school meant to me and they wanted me to glorify and praise the school. Well I wrote a speech alright but it was about my achievements and how I persevered and continued on to make it in the world. Of course they didn't like the speech and told me to change it. I said that I wouldn't because it was about my achievement at the school and in life. Needless to say, they told me in so many words that maybe I shouldn't go to the graduation. I said fine, just send me my graduation money back along with my certificate of completion. That's just what happened. The way this school draws students in is that the state that after you graduate, they will help you find a job. I went for it just like everyone else. To say the least, they never did help me find a job. I found my own job. Sometime later they called me and wanted me to go back to the school and give a speech to the new students about how I found a job and what did I have to go through to get one. Now this is the same school that didn't like my speech about perseverance within ones self. I declined and stated that my schedule was too full.

Chapter 20

NASA: Successful in All My Endeavors

I finally got a job offer from The Jet Propulsion Laboratory. I had put in an application there about the same time that I put in an application at the IRS. Of course I immediately went there to take the typing test. My typing speed was up to eighty words per minute. I had been practicing for a year on my friend's typewriter. I passed the typing test and was told that I would be hired as a Group Secretary. I was very happy that day. The section that they put me in was the Reliability Engineering Section and they just happened to use the Wang System 1140 Computer. I was very comfortable working with that computer. I was very fast at typing memos and doing corrections. The only thing that I had to learn was doing things the JPL way and that was it. I started going to a lot of their seminars at Cal Tech and at Von Karman Auditorium on Lab. My mind was beginning to expand. I read a lot of books on outer space and interplanetary travel, time travel and intergalactic travel. To me the most important question is " is there life on some other planet". My answer is yes. When I look at the way we do things here on earth and I realize that we are just a spec in the cosmos, I find it difficult to believe that we are the only ones living on a planet with a yellow sun because space is infinity with trillions of galaxies and solar systems.

I finally got the job that I wanted. I was working for NASA. To me this job was perfect. I was working for the Natural Space Environments of Reliability Engineering. I was a Group Secretary with about ten engineers in my group that I type for. I really liked working at JPL. I learned a lot there about the space program. I got to see everything first hand before the public saw it on television. I learned what it takes to travel in space and how we will live there. I learned that we are going to have to leave this planet sooner or later. The most likely place for us is the planet Mars. This planet has just about everything that we need in order to make it a terrestrial planet for us. We've already sent probes to this planet to see if there ever was life on it. Mars has polar caps, which means water and it has the minerals needed to make oxygen. We will just have to terra form it to suit us. My time working at the Lab has been very informative about the galaxy and solar system that we live in and also what it takes to colonize a planet. So I had a nice apartment in Los Feliz and I took the bus to JPL (La Canada, Flintridge) everyday and saved my money in order to buy me a car. After three to four years of saving I was able to buy me the type of car that I wanted. Not only that but I was promoted to group technical secretary.

My Life is Starting

Some times I would leave my car at home and take the bus. My plan was to save up money and use only what was needed to pay my rent and buy a little food. The rest would be saved in order to buy a house when I felt that I was ready. While working at the Lab I met a girl that worked there and she seem pretty nice and so we got together. We did a lot of talking. It seem that she wanted what I wanted, which was a good life and a nice home. So after thinking about it, I decided to move in with her. This way I could save more money and I would be helping her. The other thing is that she had two children, one boy and one girl. I thought about what it would be like living with kids. I like children and I figured that I could handle it. By moving in I immediately took responsibility of being the role model for her kids. Their father had some problems and so he was not in the picture. The children were eight years old and five years old. They were very obedient children. So now my new address became Pasadena instead of Los Feliz. Also I was very close to the lab. We all got along fine. I took the kids to the Griffith Observatory and to the zoo and basically we all had a good time. Later on I introduced them to my son and the three of them got along very well together. I didn't know that they had never been camping. So I got a couple of tents, some food, a couple of flashlights and off we went to Sequoia National Park. From Pasadena the ride was three hours long. When we arrived there I showed them how to put up the tents and how to build a fire for cooking. Everyone really enjoyed the camp out. Especially when the sun went down and we had to use the flashlights and lanterns that we brought with us. We threw a few hotdogs and stakes on the fire and the kids ate as much as they wanted and drank plenty of pop and juice. I told scary stories and only the bravest of the bunch decided to walk with me in the woods at night. After we got about one hundred yards from our campsite I stopped suddenly and said that I hear a bear coming. Every one took off running. I realized my mistake and tried to get them to stop because there was no light and they could've easily run into a tree. We all had a good laugh about it the next day. Since it was their first time being in the woods we only stay in Sequoia a day and a half but we did go back again a couple more times because everyone found out that camping can be fun. Every thing was going along fine. I liked the kids and they liked me and we were one big happy family. We decided to try and find a house for sale. At first we looked around Pasadena and found that the prices were too high. Then we found that there were a lot of vacant homes in Victorville. I didn't even know where Victorville was. As it turns out it is eighty miles north of Pasadena. Its called the High Desert. Its open area, hot and they do get snow in the wintertime. So we decided to go up there and have a look around. We had a realtor from Remax help us out. After showing us a few nice looking houses that were too small she showed us the perfect house. It was a four bedroom, two bath, two car garage for only sixty eight thousand. I used my G.I. bill and put five hundred dollars down in order to get the house. My plan was changing and I didn't want it to. A lot of things were going thru my mind. Should I or Shouldn't I. This was a big step for me. My first home and this wasn't what I had in mind. Still it seemed right. I was helping someone with kids and moving them eighty miles away from drugs and project living for a better life into a house. I thought about how I grew up and that helped me to make up my mind. So I went for it. There were still things being done to the house. They were even going to put in a brand new driveway for me and put new carpeting throughout the house. We brought the kids up to the house to see it and everyone was happy to have their own room. I allowed them to fix up their room anyway they wanted as long as it is kept clean. Of course they readily agreed. This move meant that I would be driving about one hundred and sixty miles round trip to and from JPL. I didn't mind it because I was becoming a homeowner. The air seemed to be cleaner up in Victorville. Once again things were moving the way that they should be. I had a very good job and my girlfriend (I later went to Las Vegas and married this girl) went out and got herself a good job at one of the stores in the VictorValley Mall. We both had nice cars, nice jobs and a nice home. My life was looking up. I called my sister and told her that I had just brought a four-bedroom house in the High Desert. I told her that she should come out to visit me as soon as possible. I couldn't believe that after all of the hard work those things were coming together for me after the life that I had growing up. But this was my life. I had made these things happen. Not me depending upon someone else. Everything that I had at that point I had worked and sacrificed for it to turn out the way that it did. I had made a lot of good moves (right moves) and I was proud of myself for having the stick-to-it-ness and not giving up when the going got a little tough. I do remember asking my sister for some money so that I could buy me a pair of shoes to wear to an interview because I didn't have any money. I was both happy and thankful that she sent me what I needed. I went out and brought me a pair of shoes so that I would look a little decent when I went to the interview.

The job that I got was the one at JPL. So now we're living in Victorville and it took some time getting use to the house. At first I just used it as a place to throw my clothes down and to sleep because I left early and returned home late. I really didn't do anything at the house for a while because I was too tired. Driving up and down the Cajon Pass is a job in itself. In any event we lived in that house for ten years. Then my wife decided that she wanted to go trucking. I said fine. It was good steady work plus she would be traveling all across the country. So she went to a trucking school in Rialto and they put her up in a motel. Every weekend I would go to the motel to see if she needed any money or anything before I would start up the Pass. Finally she passed her truck-driving test and got her CDL. She would be out on the road with another trucker for thirty days. I made sure that she had enough money before she got her first cheques. I was still working at JPL and holding the fort. After being on the road for thirty days, she finally got the go ahead to choose a partner. This is a male dominated industry so all that she could do was wait until someone wanted to drive with her. Then she started telling me that maybe I should do it. I said definitely no! I had a good job and was making about forty five thousand a year and I really liked my job. Then I started thinking about how it would be nice to drive across the country and see the different sights and we would be together also. The best thing about driving is that we would be making double money and the industry was looking for husband and wife teams. So against my better judgment I decided to go. Driving those big rigs is work. You have to watch what you're doing all of the time. I finally passed my truck-driving test and got my CDL. I went out for my thirty days with a very good trainer. He showed me some little tricks about driving the eighteen-wheelers. Once while going up a grade the truck just stopped because I different shift the gears fast enough. You should've heard the chatter on the CB about who is that idiot driving. Eventually I got the hang of it and I turned out to be a pretty good driver. We ran into my wife and her partner in North Platte Nebraska in the dead of winter. We might as well have been at the North Pole. It was bitter cold. The wind chill factor was about minus thirty below zero. Anyway we were happy to see each other. Finally after my thirty days we made it back to San Bernardino to the yard. My wife's truck came in a day later. We got our own Freightliner and were ready to roll. One of the things that I was told at the truck driving school was to make sure that you and your partner get along, otherwise there is going to be a problem. We got along fine except for a couple of minor problems. When we got back to San Bernardino from Carlyle Pennsylvania I decided that I didn't want to go out anymore. We finally got another job with APEX Trucking. On this job we had to drive tankers filled with cement. The job was pretty good. She had one shift and I had another. They allowed you to take the truck home with you. We even had to make a couple of trips to Las Vegas, Nevada. At one point, we thought that we could transfer to the Las Vegas yard. After checking we found out that they didn't have any openings.

Las Vegas

We moved to Las Vegas, Nevada in the year nineteen ninety-nine and for the first few months the going was tough. The weather here is very hot and dry most of the time. You have to get use to the climate. The kids were all grown and we didn't have to worry about them. We tried to give them the house in order to keep it in the family, but they didn't want it so we just let it go. Las Vegas is a gambling town. Everything here is geared toward gambling. I guess that I was fortunate to get a job with training with a good company. With this company I learned about the gaming system. I learned about the gambling machines and how to repair them. I learned about the payouts and the attitudes of different customers and how to deal with them. There are a couple of important things that I learned about Las Vegas and that is: If you win anything, cash out, if you lose anything, walk away and try some other day. If the machine says play three coins, then play three coins, if the machine says play five coins then play five coins. Do not chase any money that you have lost because you will lose more. I have seen a lot of people come to this town thinking that they are going to "hit it big" and they don't. That's why they call it GAMBLING, because you are taking a chance.

Now I am in my early fifties. I have lived a half of a century. I thought that I would never see this age. Like a lot of people, back in the fifties and early sixties I thought that by the time the year two thousand gets here we would have flying cars and would be traveling to other planets. I thought that we would've answered the question of whether or not there is life on other planets. I thought that we would have colonized Mars by now. I thought that space travel would've been the norm by now. I thought that shuttles would be going to and from the moon every day. I thought that the human race would have gotten over the fact that people are different and have different religions and think differently. I thought that by this time hunger and poverty would have been eliminated. I thought that someone from another planet would've shown us how to eliminate cancer and other diseases. I thought that the world would be introduced to alien beings from another world wanting to live among us. I thought that there would be no need for wars to be fought. As I get older I see that we may have gotten out of the cradle but we still have not stood up yet.

I wrote this book because for all of the growing teens that think that their life is hopeless, it is not. I could've given up a long time ago because I had very good reasons to just quit, but I didn't. I kept on going. This is America and in this country the way I grew up is not suppose to happen to anybody. I did not join any gangs and I did steal, but only because I was hungry or to feed my brothers. I see a lot of kids these days that just don't want to do anything hard. They want everything handed to them or they want to live for free. There is a lot more that could be said about today's society but I would like to just wait and see if and how things straighten out. **I am a product that was molded and shaped by time.** I have refused drinking, violence and other immoral ways of living. I am a successful respectable member of American society. I am A MAN and you can be one too.

A FINAL MOMENT...

My mother passed away on April 28, 2004. I did not attend her funeral.

My sister Diane passed away on May 12, 2004. I will miss my sister very much.

James